Who are the Puritans?

Who are the Puritans?

AND WHAT DO THEY TEACH?

Erroll Hulse

EVANGELICAL PRESS

EVANGELICAL PRESS
Faverdale North Industrial Estate, Darlington, DL3 0PH, England

Evangelical Press USA
P. O. Box 84, Auburn, MA 01501, USA

e-mail: sales@evangelical-press.org

web: www.evangelical-press.org

First published 2000
Second Impression 2001

British Library Cataloguing in Publication Data available

ISBN 0 85234 444 9

Printed and bound in Great Britain by CPD Wales

Contents

Part II

Help from the Puritans

List of illustrations

Acknowledgements

First, by far, I acknowledge with deepest gratitude the constant, patient and skilled help of my wife Lyn.

Appreciation is expressed to Prof. Michael Haykin for his encouragement. For inspiration in the Lord's work I thank Pastor LeeRoy Shelton Jr, Michael Snyder and the team of publishers at Chapel Library, Pensacola, Florida. The daily morning prayer meetings are the key factor in the work as a constant stream of expository materials is supplied to developing countries.

I am among many who depend upon the excellent service provided by the Evangelical Library in the West End of London and especially so in the loan of rare Puritan books. I thank the library staff.

My gratitude is recorded to Margaret Siddans for her patient proof-reading and guidance in the use of English grammar. If there are mistakes they have crept in after her correcting of the manuscript. Thanks too to Mostyn Roberts, pastor of Welwyn Evangelical Church, who read the manuscript at an early stage and made helpful suggestions.

For guidance in matters historical I express gratitude to our daughter Sharon James, to Dr Robert Oliver of Bradford on Avon, and to Iain Murray for constructive suggestions. I thank David Clark of Evangelical Press who has always encouraged me in this project.

Finally I appreciate the ministry of Dr John Armstrong, who urged me to write 'The Story of the Puritans' for the quarterly journal 'Reformation and Revival' (Spring 1996). That article formed the springboard for this book.

Erroll Hulse

Foreword

It has been rightly said that the person who has a rich appreciation of the importance of history is like the veteran traveller. Just as the traveller is able to see beyond the foibles of local custom, so the one knowledgeable in history is not easily deceived by what passes for the wisdom of the day. For the Christian this is doubly true, since God is the Lord of history. History is one of the main realms in which he delights to display his glory and teach us his wisdom. And it is in history that he is building his church, that faithful body of men and women throughout space and time. No one who claims to be part of that body should be ignorant of what God has been doing before he or she came on the scene.

But which periods in the history of the church should be studied? Well, all of them — but there are some that have richer lessons to teach Christians as they enter the third millennium since Christ's birth. The age of the Puritans must surely be reckoned one of these. Not only are there the stirring stories of men and women imprisoned and dying for their faith, but there is also the vitality and vibrancy of that faith, now found in the written records they left behind — in tracts and treatises, in sermons and diaries, in prayers and aphorisms.

We ignore the Puritans at our peril. Their firm grasp of the verities of Christianity, their commitment to seeing those truths worked out in the context of the local church and, above all, the Christ-centred passion of their spirituality, can teach us much.

To be sure, the Puritans would have us follow the example of the Bereans who examined the Scriptures every day to see if what Paul said was true (Acts 17:11). There are differences, as the three principal Puritan Confessions of Faith show. The Congregationalists in 1658 (*The Savoy Declaration*) amended some parts of the *Westminster Confession* and even added a chapter, and in 1677 the Baptists extended the chapter on the church from six paragraphs to twelve and changed the chapter on baptism.[1] But at the end of the day, when the written records of the Puritans have been tested, there is so much gold to be found that our astonishment at such riches is like what the first prospectors felt in the pioneer days of the Witwatersrand of South Africa. What riches, we are constrained to exclaim, lie in these resources of Puritanism!

It is my pleasure to recommend this new introduction to the Puritans by one who has long mined in these quarries. May the three parts of this book give us a passion for reading the Puritans and may that passion better equip us to serve and adore the God of the Puritans – Father, Son and Holy Spirit.

Michael Haykin

Introduction

The relevance of the Puritans

Who were the Puritans? When did they live? What did they accomplish? What did they teach? History is not a popular subject. We cannot assume that even those who are British are automatically well educated in the history of their own land. It is certainly rare for those outside Britain to know English history. How, then, can we introduce Christians, whether at home or overseas, to the finest theological inheritance ever?

I want to create enthusiasm for the Puritans in order to profit from their practical example and benefit from their unique balance of doctrine, experience and practice.

My concern extends beyond narrating the story. I want to create enthusiasm for the Puritans in order to profit from their practical example and benefit from their unique balance of doctrine, experience and practice. The Puritans were men of deep theological understanding and vision who prayed for the earth to be filled with a knowledge of the glory of God as the waters cover the sea.

Today missionaries are involved as never before in taking the gospel to all the world. Bible-based Christianity is spreading gradually in most of the 240 nations of the world. Believers have multiplied in great numbers, especially in sub-Saharan Africa, the Far East and South America. Teaching which engenders holy living and stability is vastly needed. Historically the Puritan epoch is best able to supply this need for they were strongest where the churches in general are weakest today.

In face of the philosophical and religious trends of today the Puritans are certainly relevant.

Postmodernism (PM)

Gradually, beginning in the 1960s and 1970s, the Western world has moved philosophically from modernism to postmodernism. For around two hundred years thinking had been shaped by the Enlightenment, with its emphasis on human reason and its optimism about human ability and human achievement. In its arrogance the modernist view bypassed God and his revelation and led to the collapse of morality.

Is Puritanism relevant within the present philosophical climate of postmodernism? Writing on the subject of PM in the Autumn 1997 issue of *Foundations*, Andrew Patterson of Kensington Baptist Church, Bristol, suggests that the Puritan approach is relevant. He maintains that 'Genuine spirituality consists in a rediscovery of the cohesive and comprehensive nature of the grace of God in the life of the believer.' This he urges, 'rejects the isolating, fracturing and compartmentalizing effects of the last two centuries, and looks back to the time of the Puritans and Pietists, when there was an approach that was far healthier, vibrant, holistic, real, scriptural and God-honouring'.

With the demise of modernism (the philosophy of the Enlightenment), we now have a vacuum. This provides us with a unique opportunity to rebuild the foundations. We are challenged to understand and apply the Word of God today. As we do so, we can look back and draw on the legacies of the Puritans. We can seek to avoid their mistakes and weaknesses, but we have a great deal to learn from their strengths. Part III examines eleven areas in which we can obtain positive help from the Puritans.

Postmodernism is fiercely antinomian. It is admitted that people make mistakes, but the word 'sin' is seldom mentioned and the idea that we all sin against God is avoided. Right and wrong are judged according to human feelings. The idea that God has an unchangeable holy moral law by which he will judge every person is unpopular. In the final chapter I have explained why we need to recapture the biblical doctrine of sin and, with help from the Puritans, have expounded that subject.

In our post-modern climate the idea that God has an unchangeable holy moral law by which he will judge every person is unpopular.

What does Puritanism have to say to the different evangelical sectors of the church worldwide today?

Neo-orthodoxy

Of the theologians classified as Neo-orthodox, Karl Barth (1886-1968) is the most significant as he, more than any other during the twentieth century, affected the course of Protestant theology in Europe and beyond. He set some on the road of studying Luther and Calvin and the Reformation of the sixteenth century. But while Barth challenged the liberal establishment, there was a failure to set the records straight with regard to liberal views of the Bible. For instance, it is absolutely vital to believe in the historicity of Adam and Eve. It is essential to endorse the supernaturalism that pervades the biblical records. With Neo-orthodoxy one is never sure about the foundations. It is like walking on sinking sand. Puritanism shares with Neo-orthodoxy the challenge to use the mind, to think and to analyse. But the strength of the Puritans is that there is never any question about the validity of the Scriptures. One walks always on the solid rock of the infallible Word of God.

The strength of the Puritans is that there is never any question about the validity of the Scriptures.

Fundamentalism

The church of Jesus Christ on earth is always wider and larger than any one segment or denomination. The evangelical movement known as Fundamentalism is only a part of the wider body. That movement gathered momentum in the 1920s and 1930s. Fundamentalists came together into a movement out of the need to combat modernist theology. The leaders drew up a list of basic truths designed to keep intact doctrines which were denied or undermined by liberals. Fundamentalism was strong in the USA and spread to other countries. The Puritans would agree with the passion to defend and promote basic truths such as the reliability of Scripture, the Trinity and the deity of Christ. Unhappily Fundamentalism added to the 'basics' a premillennial view of prophecy and in some cases Dispensationalism, which is a view of history as a series of specific time-periods. The biblical basis for these periods is tenuous, to say the least, yet the system is imposed by its propagators in an arbitrary way on the Bible. The Puritans were mostly postmillennial. A small number were premillennial. Eschatology was not made a point of division. We can learn from the Puritans not to major on minor issues. Christ's Second Coming to judgement, the end of the world, the universal physical resurrection from the dead, eternal heaven and hell are all major issues over which we cannot compromise. But, apart from a general outline, we cannot map out the future. Evangelical unity is a precious commodity and we should avoid damaging it over matters which are not central.

We can learn from the Puritans not to major on minor issues.

Fundamentalists have also been inclined to add such issues as a ban on alcohol, card-playing, tobacco, dancing and theatre-going. This has been the cause of endless strife and division. For instance, concerning alcohol, the Bible teaches temperance, not total abstinence. Wine is used at the Lord's Table. Some fundamentalists even try to change the meaning of the word 'wine' to uphold their views on total abstinence.

Puritanism is a wonderful antidote to the harmful and needless divisions which are caused by adding man-made rules to Scripture. Worldliness is an enemy. The cure is in the heart. A man can keep many rules, but be worldly still and at the same time possess a deadly spirit of Pharisaic self-righteousness. Puritanism concentrates on the great issue of the state of a person's soul. When a soul is truly joined to Christ every part of the person — his thoughts, words and actions — will be subject to the Word of God. While he make rules for his own life, he will avoid making them for others. The Puritans included a chapter in the *Westminster Confession* on the subject of Christian liberty and liberty of conscience. The Puritan message is one of liberty combined with self-control and discipline. The Puritan Confessions of Faith — Presbyterian, Congregational and Baptist — are silent where the Scripture is silent. For instance, there is nothing in the Bible about smoking, but there are passages which urge that we should care for our bodies as temples of the Holy Spirit. Liberation from harmful habits comes through the freedom imparted by Christ. That freedom comes by the inward persuasion of the Holy Spirit.

There are passages which urge that we should care for our bodies as temples of the Holy Spirit.

The New Evangelicalism

Fundamentalism has worn an angry face, being seen as fiercely separatist, intolerant and aggressive. It has been viewed as the religion of the clenched fist. It was inevitable, therefore, that more friendly and reasonable avenues of expression would be sought. This came in the form of the New Evangelicalism, with its broad, scholarly and friendly approach. However, this movement within evangelicalism has been troubled by compromise on the central issue of the inspiration and authority of Scripture. The New Evangelicalism split over the issue of the inerrancy of Scripture. Here again Puritanism is to be commended. While the Puritans could not anticipate the details of this controversy, we can appreciate the solid foundation that is laid with regard to the nature and authority of Scripture in the opening chapter of the *Westminster Confession.*

Pentecostalism

The Pentecostal movement, which is as wide and diverse as a rainbow, is noted for emphasis on three important subjects: the reality of spiritual experience, the demonstration of spiritual power, and joy in public worship. These matters were also stressed by the Puritans.

First, the Puritans placed great stress on *the spiritual experience of God's free grace in conversion*. The parameters of spiritual experience with regard to joy in justification, the love of the Father in adoption, patience in tribulation and enjoyment of Christ were explored to the full by the Puritans. The Puritan view is that we are now complete in Christ. Spiritual experience consists of the ongoing application of the believer's experimental union with the three persons of the Trinity. The New Testament does not suggest or command a specific second experience after conversion, as though something has to be added to what we already are in Christ. Many in the Pentecostal movement concede that all who are in Christ have been baptized spiritually into Christ (1 Cor. 12:12) and that no second specific experience is either mandatory or to be regarded as a type of open sesame to a Pandora's box of new experiences. The Puritans would concur that spiritual power, or the anointing of the Holy Spirit, is needed not only for preaching, but for service generally and for endurance in tribulation. The Holy Spirit is always at work in the believer to correct, guide, comfort and empower.

Secondly, there is a stress in some Pentecostal denominations on the continuation of *signs, wonders and miracles*. The Puritan view is that the apostles and prophets of the New Testament were extraordinary. They were specially endued for the work of setting the foundations. We do not have to repeat their work. It is not necessary to vindicate the Word of God with new signs and wonders. Puritan teaching is wonderfully liberating because spiritual leaders are not required to walk on water, replace missing limbs, raise the dead, or perform stupendous miracles such as creating fish and bread. The Word of God is all-sufficient and we do not need to exercise the supernatural gifts of prophecies, tongues and interpretation of tongues. As we examine the history of the Christian church through the centuries and up till the present day, the absence of miracles is evident. A major ethical embarrassment takes place when miracles are offered, especially miracles of healing, and then failure is evident. How sad it is to claim to be a miracle-worker and then disappoint the hopes of hurting people! When such promises fail disillusionment sets in which is very deep and wounding. We are not to make promises we cannot fulfil. Rather we are to point to the promise which will never fail, and that is the promise of the gospel — eternal life to everyone who repents and believes.

How sad it is to claim to be a miracle-worker and then disappoint the hopes of hurting people!

Thirdly, there is the need for *joyful public worship*. Dull, lifeless worship is a contradiction of the joy of salvation. The regulative principle is important. This is the principle by which public worship is regulated according to the specifics of the New Testament. In other words, we should engage only in spiritual worship which is specified by Scripture: the public reading of Scripture, preaching, intercessory prayer and singing. There is no specification as to how these elements are to be arranged. This suggests we have freedom in that area. There is no reason why we should not have great joy and edification in our public worship. We do not need to resort to imitating the world or to entertainment. We can combine dignity and reverence with joy and gladness.

There is no reason why we should not have great joy and edification in our public worship.

Stephen Charnock, in an exposition on John 4:24, places the focus on God as central in worship when he refers to some of the essential elements involved: 'God is a Spirit infinitely happy, therefore we must approach him with cheerfulness; he is a Spirit of infinite majesty, therefore we must come before him with reverence; he is a Spirit infinitely high, therefore we must offer up our sacrifices with deepest humility; he is a Spirit infinitely holy, therefore we must address him with purity; he is a Spirit infinitely glorious, we therefore must acknowledge his excellency ... he is a Spirit provoked by us, therefore we must offer up our worship in the name of a pacifying mediator and intercessor.'

Needless to say, tedium must be avoided in worship. The challenge for preachers not to weary their hearers will be addressed in a separate chapter on preaching.

Shallow evangelism

Possibly here more than anywhere, the Puritans can help evangelicals who use the appeal, or altar call, and who too readily pronounce people converted simply because a decision for Christ has been recorded. One of the legacies of the Puritan era is a stable doctrine of divine sovereignty and human responsibility and in this way they ensure against the errors of Arminianism, on the one hand, and Hyper-Calvinism, on the other.

Reconstructionism

This is a movement emanating from America which stresses the importance of the moral law and holds to a postmillennial position which foresees that Christianity will prevail to the point where civil governments around the world will become Christian. Reconstructionism stresses the application of biblical teaching to every facet of life, private and public, and by exposition of the Scriptures seeks to equip politicians to apply biblical law to public life. Puritanism would endorse the emphasis on the Ten Commandments and the need to persuade and teach politicians to apply these commandments in legislation. However, the Puritans would part company with any who sought to follow theonomy — that is, the application of Old Testament laws, as laid down in the Pentateuch, to public life. With regard to the future, as has already been pointed out, the Puritans varied. They were mostly postmillennial, but their optimism was centred in the transforming power of the gospel and the building up of churches, rather than preoccupation with the powers of civil government.

Broad evangelicalism

Broad evangelicalism is innocuous and is no threat to the world, to sin or the devil. The Puritans exercised spiritual power. They brought down the opposition of darkness. The English Puritans gave to England the Christian family and the Lord's Day. Allied to broad evangelicalism is impotent scholarship which is undisciplined and effete. Allied too to broad evangelicalism is shallow evangelism. In his book *Are You Really Born Again*?[1] Kent Philpott testifies as to how he has moved in his ministry from shallow evangelistic practice, with its altar call, to Reformed and Puritan practice. With regard to scholarship the Puritans were full of practical application. Sadly, often where we find substantial evangelical scholarship today, it can be lacking in the area of application.

With regard to scholarship the Puritans were full of practical application.

Calvinistic Sovereign Grace churches

Some readers may wonder what is meant by this term. The fact is that many churches disown the description 'reformed' because they disagree with the teaching on the law and the Lord's Day in the Puritan Confessions of Faith (chapters 19 and 21 in the *Westminster Confession of Faith* or its Baptist counterpart, the *1689 London Confession of Faith*.)

These churches embrace what are known as the five points of Calvinism. These five points are easily remembered by the acrostic TULIP, which stands for: total depravity, unconditional election, limited atonement, irresistible grace and perseverance of the saints. This formulation originated at the Synod of Dort in Holland in 1618-19. The five points highlight the truth that we are saved by grace alone. There are, however, dangers in a simplistic reduction of Calvinism to five points. In Scripture wherever the truth of salvation by grace alone is stated it is in the context of practical application. Without spiritual application there is the danger of being merely academic or intellectual. This was largely characteristic of fundamentalism.

As with other groupings of churches, Sovereign Grace churches vary widely in character. A few have fallen prey to a cultic spirit by implying that only those who believe in the five points are true born-again Christians. Puritanism corrects such error by keeping to the biblical centrality of union with Christ as the main feature of the Christian, a union which brings with it at one and the same time justification imputed and holiness of life shown by fruitfulness (Rom. 6:1-18). The Puritans were careful not to add to justification by faith alone. In some instances 'Calvinistic Sovereign Grace' teaching adds to justification by faith by insisting that to be a true believer a person must possess a correct understanding of the five points. But faith alone joins the believer to Christ. To that nothing must be added.

The Puritans were careful not to add to justification by faith alone.

Hyper-Calvinism

The essence of Hyper-Calvinism is to deny the common grace of the love of God to all men. In other words, it teaches that God only loves the elect and has only hatred for the non-elect. Further, Hyper-Calvinism denies the sincere free offers of the gospel to all men.

C. H. Spurgeon, although he lived in a later period of history, was a Puritan in every fibre of his being. In his preaching we have wonderful examples of the five points of Calvinism preached evangelistically. For instance, Spurgeon poured scorn on the idea of a general redemption that supposedly made salvation possible for all, but does not in fact actually save anyone. Spurgeon preached particular redemption in a most powerful evangelistic manner. The Puritans can provide stability today by the biblical manner in which they held to the different facets of the love of God and the way in which they held in harmony the doctrines of divine sovereignty and human responsibility. One example of that is John Flavel's *Christ Knocking at the Door of Sinners' Hearts,*[2] 400 pages of gripping exposition all from one text, Revelation 3:20.

The church of Christ on earth at the dawn of the twenty-first century is larger and more diverse than it has ever been. Only some aspects and strands of that huge body have been referred to in this chapter, yet from the examples quoted above it should be evident that the Puritan writings are still very relevant today.

Part I

The story of the Puritans

'Almost no one reads their writings now.' So wrote William Haller in 1957 in his book, *The Rise of Puritanism.* His comment was true then. It is not true now. Since 1957 there has taken place a Reformed theological renewal which has its roots in Puritan books.[1] In addition to the extensive publishing achievement of the Banner of Truth in the UK and *Soli Deo Gloria* publishers in the USA, there are other publishing houses in the business of reworking and publishing the Puritans.

Included in the republication of Puritan writings is the translation of Puritan expositions in other languages. For instance, Jeremiah Burroughs' *The Rare Jewel of Christian Contentment* has recently been published in Albanian, Arabic, French, Indonesian, Korean, Persian, Portuguese and Spanish.[2] The need for a popular historical background against which we can readily set the Puritan authors is one of the reasons for this presentation. I would urge newcomers to the Puritans to familiarize themselves with the names and dates of the English monarchs for the sixteenth and seventeenth centuries. The time-grid is essential. Each monarch put his or her own peculiar stamp on that part of the story. Compared with the monarchy today, the kings and queens of that era seem to have wielded supreme authority. In fact, however, their powers were ill-defined. The monarch had no standing army, was often short of money and had to govern bearing in mind the need to maintain the goodwill of the land-owning classes, who were the natural leaders in society.

A popular chart of English monarchs 1509-1702

The Tudor line

HENRY VIII (reigned 1509-1547)
Dv wife number one — Catherine of Aragon, who bore Mary, later to become queen
B wife number two — Anne Boleyn, who in 1533 bore Elizabeth, later to become queen
D wife number three — Jane Seymour who bore Edward, later to become king
Dv wife number four — Anne of Cleves; marriage supposedly not consummated
B wife number five — Catherine Howard
S wife number six — Catherine Parr
Key: DV = Divorced; B = Beheaded; D =Died;S = Survived

EDWARD VI (1547-1553) died aged only 16.
During his reign England moved politically in the direction of Protestantism.

MARY (1553-1558), nicknamed 'Bloody Mary' because of her cruelty. About 270 burned at stake for their faith. Mary married Roman Catholic Philip, son of Emperor Charles V, in 1554

ELIZABETH (1558-1603)
Principal events:
1559 The Elizabethan Settlement
1570 Elizabeth excommunicated by the pope
1588 The Spanish Armada

The Stuart line

JAMES I (1603-1625)

1604 The Hampton Court Conference

1611 Publication of the Authorized or King James Version of the Bible

1618 The Synod of Dort rejects Arminianism

1624 Richard Montagu's anti-Calvinist treatise points to the rise of Arminianism

CHARLES I (1625-1649)

1629 For eleven years Charles rules without Parliament

1637 Imposition of new Prayer Book provokes riots in Edinburgh

1640-1660 Rule by Parliament

1642 Civil War

1643-47 The Westminster Assembly

1645 Archbishop William Laud executed

1649 Charles I executed

1658 Death of Oliver Cromwell

CHARLES II (1660-1685)

1662 The Act of Uniformity and the Great Ejection of Puritan pastors

JAMES II (1685-1688)

WILLIAM III 1689-1702

In his *Short History of the English People*, J. R. Green declared, 'No greater moral change ever passed over a nation than passed over England during the years between the middle of the reign of Elizabeth and the meeting of the Long Parliament (1640-1660). England became the people of a book, and that book the Bible.'[3]

This may sound exaggerated but we can be sure that what Green meant is that the Puritans eventually came to wield a spiritual influence out of all proportion to their numbers, for they always formed a minority. It will help to see the story in perspective if we recall that the population of England in 1500 was about two million and by 1600 this had increased to approximately four million. As for religion, in spite of enforced church attendance it is doubtful whether more than a quarter of the population of England during that period could be said to have had any religion at all.[4] It is interesting to observe that, at the time of writing, the population of England is about 48 million and the country is divided into 13,000 parishes with 10,000 clergy, 8000 of whom are paid. This general observation needs to be borne in mind, not only in relation to the period under review, but even more so to the present situation, when those who profess and practise the Christian faith constitute probably less than ten per cent of the population. Ralph Josselin, in his Essex parish, did not celebrate communion for nine years and when he did, in 1651, only thirty-four qualified to take part! Josselin spoke of three categories of parishioners: first, those who seldom hear preaching; secondly, those who are 'sleepy hearers'; and third 'our society', a small group of the godly.[5]

Nominal religion has always characterized the great majority of Anglicans. It was so then as it is now. By about 1600 the number of ministers who were Puritans had increased to about ten per cent, that is, about 800 of the 8,000 Church of England clergy. By 1660 this proportion had increased to approximately twenty-five per cent. Between 1660 and 1662 around 2,000 were forced out of the national church.[6]

Before the Reformation the English church was Roman Catholic. In character it was 'a collection of practices, habits and attitudes rather than an intellectually coherent body of doctrine'.[7] The Protestantization of England was essentially gradual, taking place slowly throughout Elizabeth's reign, 'here a little and there a little', and very much in piecemeal fashion. From about 1600 onwards growth accelerated.

At the time of Henry VIII's breach with Rome England was officially completely Roman Catholic. By 1642 it is estimated that not more than two per cent were Catholics, although ten per cent of the peerage still were.

Throughout the period I will outline England was a monolithic society. Everyone was required to conform to the Church of England. This resulted in 'recusants', those who, whether because of Puritan convictions or out of loyalty to the Roman Catholic Church, refused to attend the Church of England services. From 1570 to 1791 this was punishable by a fine and involved many civil disadvantages. Recusants tended to lie low and keep out of trouble. It was during the period from 1640 to 1660 that Christian denominations surfaced: Presbyterians, Congregationalists, Baptists and Quakers (all these together representing only about five per cent of the population).[8] The Toleration Act of 1689 marked the end of the Church of England's claim to be *the* single all-inclusive Church of the English people, although it remained the church established by law.

Who were the Puritans?

In 1568 there were 'many congregations of the Anabaptists in London, who called themselves Puritans, or the unspotted lambs of the Lord'.[9] It has been widely accepted that the word 'Puritan' first came into use in connection with these groups.[10] It was during the Elizabethan period (1558-1603) that the Puritans grew increasingly as a distinct brotherhood of pastors who emphasized the great central truths of Christianity: faithfulness to Scripture, expository preaching, pastoral care, personal holiness and practical godliness applied to every area of life. The word 'Puritan' began to be used to refer to these people who were scrupulous about their way of life. 'The godly', or those who were not merely nominal, were dubbed 'Puritans'.[11] Those who cared about the gospel ('gospellers') and who sought to propagate the gospel were called 'Puritans'. As the Scriptures warn, the godly can expect to bear reproach for their holy way of life. The godly of that time were derided as killjoys and nicknamed 'Puritans'.

A new meaning of the term developed, and this came about through the Arminian/Calvinist controversy. Those ministers in England who subscribed to the doctrines of grace were called Puritans. When submitting a list of names for preferment (the ecclesiastical term for promotion) Archbishop William Laud, who was a dogmatic Arminian, placed a 'P' against the names of the Puritans, as a warning against their convictions, and an 'O' beside other names, conveying the meaning that these men were 'orthodox' (as Laud interpreted that term) and therefore acceptable.

The word 'Puritan' has been used much as a term of derision. In 1641 Henry Parker complained that 'Papists, bishops, court flatterers, stage-poets, minstrels, jesting buffoons, all the shameless rout of drunkards, lechers, and swearing ruffians, and many others took delight in deriding people as puritans.'[12]

In this section of the book I will tell the story of the Puritans under three heads: first, their antecedents; secondly, the development of the Puritan movement through the spiritual brotherhood (1558-1603); and, thirdly, the full flowering of Puritanism (1603-1662).

Antecedents of the Puritans

1. William Tyndale and the supremacy of the Bible

The first feature of the Puritan movement was a love for the Word of God. Before the rise of Puritanism ignorance of the Word of God was widespread. In 1524 William Tyndale (*c.* 1495-1536) made a brave decision to defy the laws prohibiting Bible translation and forbidding Englishmen to leave the country without permission.

Born in Gloucestershire, Tyndale was educated at Oxford, where he gained his MA in 1515. Thereafter Tyndale

William Tyndale
1495–1536

came into conflict with the local clergy, who avowed their loyalty to the pope and tradition in preference to the teachings of the Bible. Tyndale was appalled by the prevailing ignorance and in an argument with an opponent in the home of his patron Sir John Walsh at Little Sodbury in Gloucestershire asserted, 'If God spare my life, ere many years, I will cause that a boy that driveth the plough shall know more of the Scripture than thou dost.'

On the Continent Tyndale was hounded from one place to another. Eventually he was betrayed and suffered in prison. At Vilvorde near Brussels in 1536 he was put to death by strangling and burning. Thus ended the life of one of England's greatest heroes.

William Tyndale played a unique role as Bible translator and Reformer. He was martyred in the period preceding the Puritan times. This expressive portrait is by Lewis Lupton.

William Tyndale was a talented theologian. His theological writings were collected and published in 1572. Tyndale's work represents a formative contribution to the development of Protestant Christianity, especially on the central issue of justification by faith alone, by grace alone. This can be seen in his competent reply to Sir Thomas More (1478-1535), Lord Chancellor of England, who wrote books against Tyndale.

Tyndale succeeded in translating and printing the New Testament plus the Pentateuch and the book of Jonah. These translations were smuggled back into England. The ex-friar Miles Coverdale (1488-1568), an associate of Tyndale's, turned to Switzerland for protection. There, using Tyndale's work, he translated the whole Bible. Henry VIII approved this translation. By 1537 two editions had been published in England. Later the 1560 Geneva Bible became a favourite Bible with the Puritans. Between 1579 and 1615 at least thirty-nine editions of the Geneva Bible were printed in England. A predestinarian catechism was included in the Geneva Bible and there were marginal notes.[13] For instance, the locusts of Revelation 9:3 were identified as bishops and archbishops, monks and cardinals.[14]

2. The role of the martyrs and the crucial ministry of John Foxe, the martyrologist

During the short reign of Edward VI (1547-1553) the Protestant position was consolidated. However, at the death of Queen Mary (1553-1558) England was technically realigned with Rome. It was during the reign of this queen, nicknamed 'Bloody Mary', that more than 270 Protestant martyrs were burned at the stake. Included among those put to death for their faith were artisans and ordinary people, as well as leaders of great stature, such as John Bradford, and distinguished bishops, including John Hooper, Hugh Latimer, Nicholas Ridley and Thomas Cranmer, Archbishop of Canterbury.

Thus, under Mary, some of England's noblest sons lost their lives. The gruesome scenes of human bodies burning alive must have been etched into the minds of the people and no doubt were one of the primary influences in moulding the Puritans who followed, from 1558 to 1662 and beyond.

The effect of this cruelty in turning the people from Roman Catholicism to Protestantism is beyond calculation. During her reign Mary was Rome's greatest asset in England. Since her death her memory has always been Rome's greatest liability in England.[15]

The testimony of the martyrs was extraordinary. Their impact was greatly increased through the industrious writing of John Foxe.

Born in Lancashire in 1517, Foxe began studies in Oxford at the age of sixteen. His studies were instrumental in his conversion by the time he had earned his MA degree. Because of his Protestant convictions Foxe suffered acute poverty. Scholars in those days depended on wealthy patrons to give them lodging and meals in exchange for teaching services.

John Foxe

John Foxe (1517–1587)
Foxe's 'Acts and Monuments', which was the formal title given to his extensive descriptions of the martyrs, was the principal influence in turning England to Protestantism.

Unable to find such a position in London, Foxe nearly starved to death. One day he sat disconsolate in St Paul's Churchyard. A stranger came up to him and placed a generous sum of money in his hands. Three days later he obtained a position in the home of the Earl of Surrey at Reigate, where he taught the earl's children.

When Mary came to the throne, Foxe left for the Continent, where he joined English refugees, first at Frankfurt and then at Basle. He had already begun to collect materials for his work on the martyrs from the time of the apostles to those who suffered under the reign of Queen Mary. Foxe's work eventually expanded to 1,700 folio pages. Foxe was essentially a literary man, meticulous in detail. His reliability in terms of accuracy has been questioned but not refuted. A much expanded *Book of Martyrs* was published in 1570. It was placed in the cathedrals and in parish churches and in the halls of public companies.

Book of Martyrs was published in 1570.

No book ever gave such a mortal wound to Popery as this.

Never before had such a work on such a scale appeared in English, certainly never at such a moment. Daniel Neal declares, 'No book ever gave such a mortal wound to Popery as this; it was dedicated to the queen, and was in such high reputation, that it was ordered to be set up in the churches where it raised in the people an invincible horror and detestation of that religion which had shed so much innocent blood.'[16] Along with the Bible, Foxe's *Book of Martyrs* became a family book in many homes.[17]

Foxe's *Acts and Monuments* (the formal title of his extensive chronicle on the martyrs) was the principal practical means of turning England to Protestantism. The powerful testimony of the Marian martyrs in their agonizing deaths moved hearts and turned minds to consider the reasons which inspired such faith. In addition Foxe's writing was used to instil into Puritanism the ideal of the Christian hero: the person who bears faithful witness to Christ even to death. It was glorious to them that the martyrs could triumph over the last and most dreaded enemy. Dying well was part of the Puritan mentality. We see this in Bunyan's description in *Pilgrim's Progress* of the various characters who come to cross the river of death. Remember Mr Despondency? His last words were: 'Farewell night, welcome day!'

Foxe immortalized the dying sayings of the martyrs, such as Bishop Hugh Latimer's words to Bishop Ridley when they suffered together at the stake: 'Be of good comfort, Master Ridley, and play the man. We shall this day light such a candle, by God's grace, in England, as, I trust, shall never be put out.' A memorial stands at the spot in Oxford where this took place.

John Foxe inspired and promoted the idea of England as an elect nation, a people set apart from all others, a people specially called to preserve and promote the Word of God.[18]

3. The Lutheran and Genevan reformation movements, especially the example of John Calvin

Momentum for reform came to England from the writings and example of the Continental Reformers as a whole. Martin Luther (1483-1546) was the dominant early influence but later John Calvin (1509-1564) exercised a profound effect in England. Calvin's style of preaching straight through, text by text, book after book in Scripture, and his example of reformation at Geneva impressed the English refugees, of whom there were about one hundred in Geneva at the time of Mary's reign of terror. These refugees caught the vision for the complete reformation of the church, in its form of government and its form of worship. Several of these men who returned at the time of Elizabeth's accession were given high and privileged office in the Established Church. To their disappointment they realized that radical reform would be blocked.

In due course the vision of a church reformed after the Genevan pattern and made Presbyterian was taken up by Thomas Cartwright (1535-1603), a popular teacher at Cambridge. Cartwright's lectures on the Acts of the Apostles in 1570 made a tremendous impact and encouraged attempts to bring about reformation in church government. Two of his disciples, John Field and Thomas Wilcox, in 1572 wrote in detail on this theme under the title *An Admonition to Parliament*. This was forceful and uncompromising writing but exceedingly unpopular with the government. Field and Wilcox soon found themselves in prison.

When Cartwright was challenged and charged with error he answered by drawing up a statement which summarizes the issues as follows:

John Calvin

John Calvin (1509-1564) This likeness of Calvin comes from a painting found in a castle in 1955 which had upon the back in French: 'Portrait of Calvin by Holbein.' Hans Holbein (1497-1543) worked in Switzerland, Italy, France and the Netherlands, but is especially known as the court painter of King Henry VIII of England.

1. Archbishops and archdeacons (i.e. the episcopal system) ought to be abolished.
2. The officers of the church should be patterned on the New Testament model. Bishops, or elders, should preach and deacons take care of the poor.
3. Every church should be governed by its own minister and elders.
4. No man should solicit for ecclesiastical preferment.
5. Church officers should be chosen by the church and not the state.

The development of the Puritan movement

through the spiritual brotherhood (1558-1603)

When Elizabeth rode into London as queen on 23 November 1558 she was twenty-five years old. Exceptional in her ability to measure political forces, she grasped well the emotions and desires of her people. More than any other Tudor monarch, she controlled government and church policy. She spoke Latin, French and Italian fluently and could read Greek. Elizabeth resolved to work for the establishment of a strong, united nation with one united national church. William Cecil, Elizabeth's chief minister, believed that 'the state could never be in safety where there was toleration of two religions'.

Queen Elizabeth I

Queen Elizabeth I dominated England throughout her long reign. Her illustrious reign is appropriately depicted here by Lewis Lupton.

At the time of Elizabeth's accession to the throne the contest between Catholicism and Protestantism to win the hearts of the people was undecided. Most were ready to conform either way. Elizabeth's administration was moderately Protestant. She excluded fully committed Roman Catholics but neither were there any representatives of the Genevan camp. Elizabeth maintained a balance between the Roman Catholic and Protestant constituencies. Even in the matter of marriage she kept everyone guessing. Marriage to a foreign prince would have enormous political and religious implications. In the event she never married. She was less violent than her half-sister Mary. Nevertheless at least two Anabaptists were burned at the stake in 1575 and separatist leaders such as Greenwood, Barrowe and Penry were executed by hanging in 1593.

The pope excommunicated Queen Elizabeth in 1570. This strengthened opposition to the pope and assisted the Protestant cause in England. In 1588 a massive effort was made by Spain to invade England. The Spanish Armada consisted of an impressive fleet of 130 ships intended to convey 50,000 soldiers as an attacking force. The Armada suffered an overwhelming defeat. Less than half the Spanish ships returned home. This event further strengthened the Protestant party in England since the English, then as now, prize their nationhood. They resented the threat from Roman Catholic Spain, a nation notorious for the Inquisition, a most hideous and devilish system of persecution.

To appreciate the conditions under which the brotherhood of godly Puritan pastors laboured it is important to understand the Acts of Supremacy and Uniformity and the new Prayer Book which were imposed upon England in 1559. The effect of the Act of Supremacy was to declare Elizabeth to be 'Supreme Head of the Church of England', thus ensuring that the Church of England was never free from the control of the royal government up to 1640.

The way in which we worship God is a sensitive issue and it is not surprising that pressure for ministers to wear the surplice (a loose white over-garment) caused resentment. Most conformed for the sake of peace. Others refused. A Manchester curate preached that 'The surplice is a rag of the pope and a mighty heresy in the church and he who maintains it cannot be saved!' A minister appearing before the Bishop of Lichfield in 1570 called it 'a polluted and cursed mark of the beast' and warned that thanks to the use of 'such rags of antichrist', the people 'will fall away from God into a second popery that will be worse than the first!'[19]

The application of the laws enforcing conformity varied from place to place. Many bishops had little desire to persecute ministers who were, after all, fellow-Protestants.

The inception of the Puritan movement is found in a spiritual fellowship of gifted pastors/preachers that emerged in the 1580s and 1590s. Some of the best known were Richard Greenham, Henry Smith, Richard Rogers, Laurence Chaderton, Arthur Hildersam, John Dod, John Rogers and William Perkins. Puritans multiplied through the work of these leaders who became famous, not only for their preaching, but as physicians of the soul. I will describe briefly four of these leaders of the brotherhood.[20]

1. Richard Greenham (1531-1591)

In 1570 Greenham left the academic atmosphere of Cambridge, where he had been a tutor, to take up pastoral work in the humble village of Dry Drayton about five miles from Cambridge. There he laboured for twenty years, only occasionally preaching away from home. Greenham was a pastor *par excellence*, a physician able to discern the deep experiences of the soul, an expert in counselling and comforting. He constantly rose, winter and summer, at 4 a.m. He refused several lucrative offers of promotion and abounded in acts of generosity to the poor.

Young men came to live at Dry Drayton, forming a 'School of Christ' and devoting themselves to the Scriptures and to the outworking of the Word in their own souls and the souls of others. Why should a village situation be exciting? The answer is that here we see a microcosm of a wider work, the rooting of the gospel in rural England. Richard Greenham was criticized for his nonconformity and the manner in which he conducted worship services. He was passive in his resistance. He did not wish to argue about things he regarded as *adiaphora*, that is, things indifferent. He preached Christ, and him crucified, and simply pleaded for tolerance that he should continue to be a faithful minister of Christ. He enjoyed the friendship of men of influence who always managed to put in a good word for him and thus keep him out of trouble.

2. Richard Rogers
(1550-1620).

In 1574 Richard Rogers became a preacher of God's Word in the village of Wethersfield, Essex, there to labour for the conversion of souls, but also to work at the mortification of sin in his own soul. Like Greenham, he kept a school for young men in his house.

Having first committed himself to the rigours of the godly life, he wrote in detail on practical godly living. This was called *The Seven Treatises*, a work which went through seven editions before 1630. His close friend and neighbour Ezekiel Culverwell expressed the wish that readers of the book could have seen its author's practice with their own eyes and heard his doctrine with their own ears. Here we see illustrated a fascination with the essence of godliness. Rogers kept a diary and from it can be seen a man walking as closely as possible with God. One of his series of expositions gained fame, namely, discourses on the book of Judges.[21]

We should not imagine that Rogers led an easy life, being waited on by servants, so that he could give himself to spiritual exercises. Besides the care of his immediate large family we read of him

Richard Rogers

Richard Rogers (1550-1620) Having first committed himself to the rigours of the godly life, Richard Rogers wrote a treatise on practical godly living. This was called The Seven Treatises, a work which went through seven editions before 1630. His close friend and neighbour Ezekiel Culverwell expressed the wish that readers of the book could have seen its author's practice with their own eyes and heard his doctrine with their own ears.

that 'He did regard it as his duty to meditate, study and write but at the same time he carried on no less conscientiously the activities of a householder, a farmer, a figure in the countryside, a preacher, a pastor, a reformer and the head of a boarding school.'

3. William Perkins (1558-1602)

William Perkins laboured at Cambridge with remarkable effect. Combined in him, to a remarkable extent, were the spiritual qualities and ministerial skills typical of the brotherhood. He excelled both in the pulpit and with the pen, keeping the university printer busy with many books. More than those of any other minister of his time, his published works were found on the shelves of the generation that followed him. He was the first to write a full exposition on the subject of preaching in *The Art of Prophesying.*[22] Perkins' approach to preaching was essentially applicatory, and in this he was typical of the Puritans. In preparation he considered the needs of every kind of hearer in the congregation. His writings exceeded in quantity and quality all other Puritan authors up to that time.

William Perkins

William Perkins (1558-1602). Perkins excelled both in the pulpit and with the pen, keeping the university printer busy with many books. More than those of any other minister of his time, his published works were found on the shelves of the generation that followed him. He was the first to write a full exposition on the subject of preaching with the title 'The Art of Prophesying'. Typical of the Puritans, Perkins made sure that he applied Christian doctrine to practical living.

William Perkins was no ivory-tower academic. For example, he made it his business to obtain permission to minister to the prisoners in jail. He won souls to Christ from among them, just as he did among the huge crowds who came to hear him preach at St Andrew's. It is said of him that his sermons were, at one and the same time, all law and all gospel: all law to expose the shame of sin, and all gospel to offer a full and free pardon for lost sinners. His was an awakening ministry which stirred lost souls to see the reality of eternal condemnation. Perkins was so gifted in eloquence that it was said that the very way he uttered the word 'damn' made sinners tremble.

Perkins died young. His loss was sorely felt.

4. Laurence Chaderton (1537-1635)

Laurence Chaderton, on the other hand, lived to be almost a hundred years old and published little. He came from a wealthy Roman Catholic family by whom he was 'nuzzled up in Popish superstition'. He suffered disinheritance when he embraced the gospel and Puritanism. A well-known benefactor of that time was Sir Walter Mildmay, who founded Emmanuel College at Cambridge. Sir Walter chose Chaderton to be master of that college, a position which he filled for forty years. He was a lecturer for fifty years at St Clement's Church, Cambridge. When he eventually came to give up his lectureship at St Clement's, forty ministers begged him to continue, claiming that they owed their conversion to his ministry. There is a description of him preaching for two hours, after which he announced that he would no longer trespass on his hearers' patience, whereupon the congregation cried out, 'For God's sake, sir, go on! Go on!'

The role of universities, lectureships and 'prophesyings'

The growth of Puritanism was due to pastors of this kind whose lives and godly example captured the imagination of many. However, as we have seen in the case of William Perkins and Laurence Chaderton, the role of Cambridge University was tremendous in advancing Puritanism. Puritan-endowed colleges such as Emmanuel and Sidney

Sussex produced a steady supply of talented Puritan pastors and preachers.

In tracing the rise of Puritanism we must reckon too with the role of lectureships. In market towns magistrates engaged their own preachers and organized weekday sermons. Lectureships were established which were a means of bypassing the system of conformity to the Prayer Book and church ceremonial. Richard Rogers of Wethersfield, Essex, and Henry Smith at St Clement Danes in London officially acted as lecturers. Between 1560 and 1662 at least 700 clergymen held lectureships at one time or another in London. Of these at least sixty per cent were Puritans.[23] The patronage of nobles and gentry played an important role in the advance of the Puritan movements. Wealthy patrons supported and protected Puritan preachers.

During Elizabeth's reign the place of 'prophesyings' loomed large. These were meetings for preaching expository sermons and discussion which became very popular. Elizabeth felt threatened and sought to suppress these meetings. Archbishop Edmund Grindal refused to carry out her will and argued in favour of the prophesyings. For his faithfulness he was suspended from office for the last seven years of his life and confined to his house for most of that time. In May 1577 the queen herself sent letters to the bishops ordering them to suppress the prophesying meetings.

The full flowering of Puritanism (1603-1662)

This period from 1603 to 1662 was turbulent, a time when conflict between Crown and Parliament came to a climax in the civil war. Religious pluralism surfaced in the 1640s. The story of the Puritans reached its apex in this period, especially as it is seen in the Westminster Assembly. It is vital to know the history which I will now sketch in five phases: firstly, the reign of James I; secondly, Charles I and Archbishop Laud; thirdly, the Civil War and the rise of Oliver Cromwell; fourthly, the period of Puritan ascendancy; fifthly, the restoration of the monarchy and the decline of Puritanism.

James I

This portrait of James I is by Lewis Lupton

1. The reign of James I

Elizabeth 1 died in 1603. She had purposed to make England great, and in that she saw a considerable measure of success. Despite her personal tantrums, sulks and at times irrational behaviour, her reign was a period of political stability, especially viewed in the light of what was to follow in the mid-seventeenth century.

As already noted, at the beginning of the seventeenth century the Puritans represented about ten per cent of the body of Church of England clergy. The Puritans fostered high hopes that the new king (James VI of Scotland, James I of England), coming from Presbyterian Scotland, would herald church reform. They were sadly disappointed.

A petition known as the Millenary Petition, believed to represent about 1,000 Puritans, was presented to James I on his way from Scotland to London. This petition urged reformation and led to the conference known as the Hampton Court Conference. This took place on three separate days in January 1604 at Hampton Court Palace in London. James was highly intelligent. He understood well the intricacies of church government. He believed in the 'divine right of kings', which meant that he had a God-given right to rule and that to disobey the king was to disobey God. James had every intention of maintaining supreme power, having had enough of cantankerous Presbyterians in Scotland. It was clear as daylight that the Puritans wished to introduce Presbyterianism into the Church of England. As the Hampton Court Conference went on, so King James became more and more bad-tempered. He made dogmatic assertions such as, 'No bishop, no king!' and 'Presbytery agrees as much with monarchy as God with the devil!' And to the Puritan divines he said, 'You had better hurry up and conform, or you will be harried out of the land!' The conference ended in a right royal flurry of bad temper! The king was agreeable to a new translation of the Bible being undertaken. This is the version we know as the Authorized Version, or King James Version, which was completed in 1611. Otherwise concessions were few and insignificant.

Between 1604 and 1609 about eighty clergy were deprived of their livings on the grounds of their nonconformity, most of these before 1607. The bishops had been told to persuade, rather than coerce, subscription to Anglican practice. In Parliament the godly campaigned for the reinstatement of deprived ministers.[24]

King James sent delegates to Dort. Held in 1618-19 in the Netherlands, the Synod of Dort was an important event in the history of the Christian church. The conference affirmed the orthodox Calvinist position on the sovereignty of God over against the tenets of Arminianism. James supported the Calvinist position against the Arminians. Subsequently he became ambivalent on the issue. In 1624 Richard Montagu published an anti-Calvinist treatise with the title *A New Gagg for an Old Goose*. This was part of an increasing trend towards Arminianism in the national church.[25]

2. Charles I and Archbishop Laud

James I died in 1625. Charles I, handsome, dignified and chaste, was enthroned king. However, unlike Elizabeth and his father James, he lacked political skill, especially in the

Charles I

This likeness of King Charles I was drawn by Lewis Lupton

art of keeping checks and balances which is so essential in politics.

Charles married Henrietta Maria, sister of the reigning French king, Louis XIII. Henrietta Maria was an ardent Roman Catholic. She meddled with state affairs. This created constant suspicion among members of Parliament and in the nation. These suspicions were mixed with fear as the cause of Protestantism on the continent of Europe was receding, a situation which placed many Protestants in danger.

William Laud

Archbishop William Laud (1573-1645)
Of all the archbishops of the Anglican Church, Laud departed the furthest from the principles of the Reformation and drew nearest to the Roman Catholic Church. He encouraged the reintroduction of stained-glass windows, crosses, crucifixes and railed altars.

William Laud became Charles's trusted adviser. From the time of the accession of Charles to the throne in 1625, Laud was exercising power, but this was formalized when he became archbishop in 1633. James had warned Charles that Laud did not understand the Scottish people: 'He kenned not the stomach of that people.' This was a warning which Charles did not heed. Laud was hostile in every way to the Puritan teaching. One of his first acts as archbishop was to encourage games and pastimes on the Lord's Day, which antagonized the Puritans. He was an avowed supporter of Arminianism, with its emphasis on free will and rejection of predestination. Laud was superstitious. He embraced the outward forms of Roman Catholic worship but rejected the authority of the pope. His idea of what he called 'the beauty of holiness' consisted of rituals and ceremonies. To this day many Anglican churches have altars at the east end. Although the canon law always refers to 'the holy table', the idea of the altar is perpetuated. The message of an altar is that of sacrifice. Laud believed the altar was 'the greatest place of God's residence upon earth — yea, greater than the pulpit'.[26]

The famous historian Lord Thomas Macaulay (who did not comprehend the spirituality of the Puritans) certainly had the measure of William Laud and wrote of him, 'Of all the prelates of the Anglican Church, Laud had departed farthest from the principles of the Reformation, and had drawn nearest to Rome... He was by nature rash, irritable, quick to feel for his own dignity, slow to sympathize with the sufferings of others, and prone to the error, common in superstitious men, of mistaking his own peevish and malignant moods for emotions of pious zeal. Under his direction every corner of the realm was subjected to a constant and minute inspection. Every little congregation of separatists was tracked out and broken up...'[27] Macaulay's hyperbole accurately depicts the zeal of the persecutors but we can be thankful that by no means all separatist assemblies were broken up.

As archbishop, Laud wielded power to arrest and imprison those who would not conform. He used a court called the Star Chamber to interrogate and persecute. An example of the cruelty of Laud is seen in the case of Dr Alexander Leighton, father of the well-known archbishop Robert Leighton. Without any defence or right of appeal, Leighton was sent to Newgate Prison. When brought before an arbitrary court he was condemned to have his ears cut off and his nose slit on both sides, to be branded in the face with the letters 'SS' (for 'Sower of Sedition'), to be twice whipped, to be placed in the pillory and then to be subject to life imprisonment! When this outrageous sentence was pronounced Laud gave thanks to God![28] Other well-known characters who received similar barbaric treatment were William Prynne, John Bastwick, Henry Burton and John Lilburne.

Bitter persecution was waged against the Puritans. Between 1629 and 1640, 20,000 men, women and children left for New England, including seventy-nine ministers, twenty-eight of whom returned when conditions improved at home.[29] Many made their exodus through the Netherlands. Among the most famous leaders to settle in New England were Thomas Hooker, John Cotton and Thomas Shepard. The role of William Ames (1576-1633) is noteworthy. He was a Puritan whose ministry was principally exercised in Holland. His writings were very popular in New England. *The Marrow of Theology* was his most influential book.

Charles ruled the country without Parliament from 1629 to 1640. Administration was maintained through county courts. Political power lay largely in the hands of about sixty noblemen, or peers, very wealthy aristocrats who owned most of the land. Below them were the gentry. When the Civil War began in earnest in 1642 peers and gentry were more or less evenly divided in their loyalties to the king.

3. Civil War and the rise of Oliver Cromwell

When Laud attempted to enforce the Church of England Prayer Book and Liturgy on Presbyterian Scotland in 1638, it was like striking a match to dry gunpowder! This is highlighted by a famous incident in St Giles Church, Edinburgh. Infuriated by a pompous dean in a white surplice walking down the aisle to announce the reading, Jenny Geddes took hold of her stool and hurled it at him! Translated into modern English, she cried out, 'You miserable upstart! Will you say mass in my ear?' Jenny's example greatly heartened others to resist the imposition of Roman Catholic rituals which they hated.

In 1638 Charles mobilized an army to subdue Scotland but the English army was soundly defeated and in 1639 a truce was negotiated.

Tensions between Parliament and the king increased. Demonstrations in London against royal authority and popery were quickly put down. The king tried to assert his own authority over Parliament. On 4 January 1642, with a band of armed men, he entered the House of Commons in order to arrest the leader of Parliament, John Pym, and four other leaders. This backfired. The five had been forewarned. Just in time they escaped by barge down the River Thames and hid in the city. This action by the king incited much more opposition to himself. A revolution was brewing. For his own safety Charles was obliged to leave London. By May 1642 he had set up his headquarters in York.

Map of England at the time of the Civil War drawn by John Woodcock. From The English Civil War: A Concise History, by Maurice Ashley, published by Thames and Hudson Ltd, 1974.

The first battle of the civil war which ensued took place at Edgehill in October 1642. This resulted in a draw. At first there seemed to be a balance of power between the Royalists (Cavaliers) and the parliamentary forces (Roundheads). In an attempt to break what was a military deadlock Parliament signed the Solemn League and Covenant with the Scots.

In January 1644 a Scottish army crossed the border. In July 1644 the battle of Marston Moor was fought and won by the combined armies of Scotland, Yorkshire (led by Sir Thomas Fairfax) and the Eastern Association (led by Oliver Cromwell and the Earl of Manchester). It was Oliver Cromwell's role and success in this battle that created his military reputation and won his soldiers the nickname 'Ironsides'.

This victory was not followed up. Some of the Parliamentary leaders, especially the Earl of Essex, were weak and indecisive. Parliament realized that a more determined and resolute leadership was needed. Victory could not be achieved without better generals and the reorganization of the army. Cromwell blamed one of the leaders, the Earl of Manchester, for retreating instead of attacking the enemy. Manchester made a reply which is very revealing because it shows what was at stake if the Roundheads were to lose this war to the Cavaliers: 'If we beat the King ninety-nine times yet he is King still, and his posterity, and we are his subjects still; but if the King beat us *once* we should be hanged and our posterity undone.'

In 1645 the army was reorganized as the New Model Army. The commander-in-chief was Sir Thomas Fairfax, only thirty-three years old. His cavalry general was Cromwell. In the Civil War battles from this point forward it was Cromwell's military discipline and strategies that proved decisive. Lord Macaulay describes Oliver Cromwell as one who feared God and was zealous for public liberty. He writes, 'With such men he filled his own regiment, and, while he subjected them to a discipline more rigid than had ever before been known in England, he administered to their intellectual and moral nature stimulants of fearful potency... Fairfax, a brave soldier, but of mean understanding and irresolute temper, was the nominal Lord General of the forces; but Cromwell was their real head... Cromwell made haste to organize the whole army on the same principles on which he had organized his own regiment... That which chiefly distinguished

Oliver Cromwell

(1599–1658)

Cromwell was given the title of Lord Protector. He was motivated not by personal ambition but by his Christian faith. This extraordinary leader has been criticized for paying too much attention to feelings while at prayer and for his tendency to interpret success as necessarily a sign of divine approval. However his sober judgement is seen in his choice of John Owen, Joseph Caryl, Thomas Goodwin and John Howe as his chaplains. In an excellent summary of Cromwell Michael Boland declares, 'Oliver Cromwell's religious integrity and practical wisdom saved the Puritan revolution from sterility and self-destruction. He struck lasting blows against tyranny and clericalism in England, and his rule made English Puritanism famed and respected in his day and to succeeding generations' (Encyclopaedia of Christianity, Jay Green, 1972).

The portrait: Collection of Buccleugh and Queensbury. From The English Civil war: A Concise History, by Maurice Ashley, published by Thames and Hudson Ltd, 1974.

the army of Cromwell from other armies was the austere morality and the fear of God which pervaded all ranks. It is acknowledged by the most zealous Royalists that in that singular camp no oath was heard, no drunkenness or gambling was seen, and that during the long dominion of the soldiery, the property of the peaceable citizen and the honour of women were held sacred.'[30]

Cromwell surrounded himself with men of prayer. He led his men into battle. He possessed an astonishing ability to measure the morale of his soldiers and knew just the right moment to strike for victory. Cromwell fought many battles and never lost one. When we remember that he did not train in a military academy, but was his own architect in warfare, he must go down in history as one of the greatest generals of all time. Roman Catholic author Lady Antonia Fraser, in her biography,[31] says of Cromwell as a strategist: 'To achieve what was necessary to do, and achieve it perfectly is a rare distinction whatever the scale: it is that which gives to Cromwell, him too, the right to be placed in the hall of fame.'

4. The period of Puritan ascendancy

Archbishop Laud was imprisoned by Parliament in 1641 and executed for treason by beheading at the Tower of London in January 1645. Government of the church by bishops was abolished in 1646. Progressive victory for Parliament in the war brought a new set of problems. There was a division in Parliament between the Presbyterians and the Independents. The Presbyterian majority in Parliament disliked and feared the army, in which the Independents dominated. There was unrest in the army due to unpaid wages. In 1647 Charles negotiated a secret treaty with the Scots which led to a renewal of civil war. Charles's duplicity led to the army bringing him to trial and on January 1649 he was executed as a traitor to the Commonwealth of England.

Charles II was recognized as king in Scotland. The army supporting him was defeated by Cromwell at the battle of Dunbar in 1650. Exactly a year later armies in favour of Charles II were routed by Cromwell at Worcester. That victory for Parliament brought the Civil War to an end. Charles II escaped to France. Cromwell became the Lord Protector and ruled through Parliament. He was a firm believer in religious liberty and was, in that respect, ahead of his times.

The House of Commons
From an engraving by John Glover. Reproduced by permission of the British Museum.
From the time of the civil wars Parliament has prevailed as the dominant power in the British constitution

On 12 June 1643, Parliament passed an ordinance calling for an assembly of learned and godly divines for the settling of the government and liturgy of the Church of England. On 1 July the Westminster Assembly convened, the first of 1163 meetings until February 1649. There were 151 nominated members, 121 of whom were ministers and 30 laymen.

The assembly completed the *Westminster Confession of Faith*, the *Larger and Shorter Catechisms* and the *Directory of Public Worship*. The influence of these materials, particularly the Confession of Faith, on subsequent generations around the world has been immense. Congregationalists in 1658 and Baptists in 1677 embraced the same basic confession, each making amendments which would constitute about ten per cent of the whole.

The depth and quality of leadership among Puritan pastors in the mid-seventeenth century is unique in the history of Christ's church in England. Some of the better-known Puritans of this time were Robert Bolton, Robert Harris, Jeremiah Burroughs and William Gouge. Among the more famous Puritans who lived through the period 1640-1660 and beyond whose entire works have been republished in entirety or substantially in modern times are Thomas Goodwin, Thomas Manton, Stephen Charnock, John Owen, Richard Baxter, John Bunyan, John Flavel, William Bridge, David Clarkson, George Swinnock, Richard Sibbes and John Howe. Of the leaders involved in the Westminster Assembly William Gouge is one of the best known. He sustained the longest and most powerful ministry, possibly ever, in the history of London. Edmund Calamy, whom some esteemed as the leader of the Presbyterian party, stands out. He preached frequently to Parliament. Hanserd Knollys and Henry Jessey were Baptists. Their biographies have inspired Baptists in recent years.[32] In addition to the immortal works of John Bunyan, *The Pilgrim's Progress* and *The Holy War*, there are many famous books which continue to be republished. Thomas Watson's *Body of Divinity* is one example and Baxter's *Reformed Pastor* is another.[33]

5. The restoration of the monarchy and the decline of Puritanism

In 1658 Cromwell died. It was soon evident that Richard Cromwell could not fill the leadership role vacated by his father. To avoid further upheaval the option to restore the monarchy was pursued. At Breda in Holland Charles II promised to respect tender consciences. When he came to power that desire was soon overruled by fierce urges for revenge among the Anglicans who now had the upper hand. From 1643 to 1654 about thirty-four per cent of the 8,600 parish clergy had suffered harassment of some kind as well as ejection, sometimes for incompetency but also for giving support to the royalist cause or for popery.[34]

In January 1661 Thomas Venner, a leader of the Fifth Monarchy movement, became prominent. He had on a previous occasion been arrested for planning an insurrection against Cromwell and had been spared execution. Led by Venner, about fifty followers terrorized parts of London. Twenty-two people were killed. Wild elements and civil disorders by fanatics of this kind provided the ruling Anglicans with an excuse to apply stern measures. They did not discriminate. Anarchy provided an excuse for the authorities to clamp down on all nonconformists. In vain the Baptists dissociated themselves from Venner. On 10 January 1661 a royal proclamation was passed forbidding all meetings of 'Anabaptists, Quakers, and Fifth Monarchy men'. Within a short time over 4,000 Quakers were imprisoned. Armed soldiers dragged Baptists out of their beds at night and thrust them into prison. This was the time when Bunyan spent twelve years in prison. He survived. Many did not.

There followed legislation against all forms of nonconformity known as the Clarendon Code, so named after the Earl of Clarendon.

In 1662 an act was passed which required strict conformity to the Church of England. If clergymen had not been episcopally ordained they were required to submit to a ceremony of reordination. Assent was required to every part of the *Book of Common Prayer*. Every minister was required to take an oath of canonical obedience and to renounce the Solemn League and Covenant.

These demands had a devastating effect on the Puritans whose consciences could not submit to the conditions imposed. Estimates vary, but it is reckoned that about 2,000 were forced out of their livings.[35] Included were some men who held teaching posts. We can only guess how many Puritans chose to remain in the national church in spite of the pressures to conform.[36] Included among those who remained was the famous William Gurnall, author of *The Christian in Complete Armour.*

1662 marks the beginning of decline for the English Puritans. The period which follows is known as the era of 'Dissent'. The last well-known Puritans to pass from this world were John Howe, who died in 1705, and Thomas Doolittle, who died in 1707.[37]

1662, then, is an important turning-point in the story of the Puritans. The influence of their preaching waned from that point onwards, but their writing ministry continued. Some of the most valuable Puritan treatises were penned in the post-1662 period. An example is that of John Owen, whose monumental commentary on Hebrews, his book on indwelling sin and his exposition of Psalm 130 were all written after 1662. John Owen deserves the title 'Prince of the Puritans'. His entire works of twenty-five volumes probably constitute the best repository of reliable theology in the English language. He is viewed as *the* theologian of the Puritan movement.[38]

Why did the Puritan movement decline sharply after 1662? Persecution of Dissenters was severe and relentless. Nonconformists were barred from the universities and this had an adverse effect on the standards of the ministry. The cogent spiritual unity that had been characterized and encouraged by the growing spiritual brotherhood of the Puritan pastors during the reign of Elizabeth and that had flowered in the ascendant Puritan movement which followed declined after 1662. In 1672 the king issued a Declaration of Indulgence which for a short time eased the lot of Dissenters and Roman Catholics.

One of the principal reasons for the decline of the Puritan movement was their loss of unity. Dr Lloyd-Jones placed the main blame on the Presbyterians. Instead of holding fast to the unity spelled out so clearly in passages like John 17, Presbyterian leaders resorted to political expediency. They lost sight of spiritual constraints.[39]

A further reason contributing to the decline of Puritanism in the latter part of the seventeenth century is the fact that when the famous leaders whose books we enjoy today passed on there were very few of similar calibre to take their place.

An explanation of the Puritan story

In an article published in the *Evangelical Quarterly* in 1980 Jim Packer described Puritanism as a movement of revival.[40] He carefully defined what he meant as revival. I would argue that, measured in terms of the eighteenth-century awakening, the story of the Puritans as I have outlined it was not a revival in spectacular 'Whitefieldian' fashion. There were some remarkable preachers, like Richard Baxter, John Bunyan and John Rogers, and lesser-known pastors, such as Samuel Fairclough of Kedington, not far from Cambridge, and his son Richard Fairclough of Mells, a village in Somerset, men with powerful awakening ministries who reaped rich harvests. But it would be difficult to show that this was typical of all the Puritans.

The explanation of the story of the Puritans is that here we have a race of preachers/pastors who believed in expounding and applying the whole counsel of God's Word with all the hard work that requires. This was a labour in which they sought the closest conjunction of the Holy Spirit with the Word.[41] Sometimes to a greater, sometimes to a lesser extent, the Holy Spirit did breathe upon the Word and he breathed new life into dead souls. The Puritans did not seek a new age of wonders, signs and miracles. Their view was that a church rises or falls as the ministry of the Word rises or falls in that church.[42] Essentially they believed in breaking up fallow ground. In this general character the Puritans are an example to every succeeding generation of pastors, whether they be pastors labouring at home or in remote areas where the indigenous people are receiving the Word for the first time.

The legacy of the Puritans

As we view the whole story of the Puritans in perspective I will point to three Puritans who lived at the time when the movement was at its height and offer a definition of what Puritanism means for the present day: Puritanism is John Owen for profundity and reliability in theological formulation, Richard Baxter for evangelistic and pastoral zeal and John Bunyan for compelling, powerful preaching. Note how different these three were. This is a reminder that, for the most part, the mainline Puritans were tolerant over differences, whereas evangelicals today are not.

The Church of England has never recovered from the Ejection of 1662. From time to time there have been exceptional leaders like Bishop J. C. Ryle (1816-1900). Ryle followed the emphases of the Puritans and wrote in their style. His well-known book with the title *Holiness* is typical and expounds the Puritan doctrine of progressive sanctification. Enthusiasm for Puritanism is rarely found in the Church of England.

The legacy of Puritan theology and devotion has from time to time given birth to extraordinary preachers and leaders. Such was Charles Haddon Spurgeon, who is correctly described as an heir of the Puritans.

Another heir of Puritanism is Dr Martyn Lloyd-Jones, who recommended Puritan books and followed them in his theology and style of expository preaching. In his leadership of pastors Dr Lloyd-Jones resembled the founders of Puritanism, Richard Greenham, John Dod and Laurence Chaderton. As in the case of the leading Puritans, Dr Lloyd-Jones' pulpit ministry formed the basis of his writings which have been influential round the world.

The Puritan testimony of godliness and sound doctrine is more relevant than ever as we find ourselves in a new millennium. The English Puritans gave England the Christian family and the Lord's Day. They were balanced Calvinists and left us an example of a stable doctrine of divine sovereignty and human responsibility. Preserved through their writings is the biblical doctrine of sin which in this era of postmodernism we are in danger of losing entirely. Added to this was their view of the moral law as binding, not for salvation, but as a principle of conduct for the regenerated heart to glorify God in the obedience of faith. The Puritans call us to a robust prayer and devotional life. They remind us of the importance of keeping the heart with all diligence and of the reality of spiritual warfare and the need to be watchful.

The Puritan hope for the future growth of the church was God-centred and founded on promises that cannot fail. The Puritan doctrine of the last things inspired prayer, motivated effort, inculcated endurance and strengthened patience. One of the first to implement this outlook in practice was the Puritan John Eliot. In 1631, at the age of twenty-seven, he sailed for Massachusetts. He became pastor of a new church a mile from Boston. Burdened for the Indian tribes, he set himself to master the Algonquin language. He began at the age of forty and eventually translated the entire Bible into Algonquin. Converts were made, churches planted and Indian pastors trained. By the time of his death aged eighty-four there were many Indian churches.

Puritanism is eminently biblical and balanced in its proportion of doctrine, experience and practical application. For that reason it is very attractive to the godly. Of its future place in the world who can tell? If the mainline Puritans were correct in their biblical optimism we can be assured that the whole earth will be filled with a knowledge of Christ's glory as the waters cover the sea (Hab. 2:14) and, as the prophet declares, 'My name will be great among the nations, from the rising to the setting of the sun. In every place incense and pure offerings will be brought to my name, because my name will be great among the nations, says the LORD Almighty' (Mal. 1:11).

Part II

The lives of the Puritans

Against the background of the overview of the history of the Puritan era given in Part I, I now present some short biographical sketches. Two factors dominate the choice of subjects. The first is to become acquainted with those Puritans whose writings have been republished. Who were these preachers and what were they like? The second is to capture the character of the movement through some of the leaders who, while not known for their writings, made an impact in other ways. Benjamin Brook provides brief sketches of the lives of about 450 Puritans in his three volumes. Here I will introduce two Reformers, five Elizabethan Puritans, five pre-1662 Puritans and twelve who lived through the climactic ejection of 1662 and beyond. In this way we will keep in step with the story already told and seek to enter into more of the struggles of these ministers of the gospel and to gain an appreciation of the inheritance they have left us by the example of their godly lives and in their expository writings.

Forerunners of the Puritans

As we have seen, antecedent to the great Puritan movement was the Reformation. From among many martyrs, including prominent leaders such as Bishops Hugh Latimer,

Time chart – Illustrating the Puritan era.

1500	10	20	30	40	50	60	70	80	90	1600	10	20	30	40	50	60	70	80	90	1700	10

Reign of: *Henry VIII* | *E* | *M* | *Elizabeth* | *James I* | *Charles I* | *Inter-Reg* | *Charles II* | *J* | *William III*

Archbishops of Canterbury

William Warham | Thomas Cranmer | P | Matthew Parker | G | John Whitgift | B | George Abbot | William Laud | Gilbert Sheldon | William Sancroft

William Tyndale

John Hooper

John Bradford

John Foxe

Richard Greenham

Laurence Chaderton

John Dod

Richard Rogers

William Perkins

Richard Sibbes

William Gouge

Jeremiah Burroughs

Henry Jessey

Thomas Goodwin

Thomas Manton

Thomas Watson

John Owen

Richard Baxter

John Bunyan

John Howe

1500	10	20	30	40	50	60	70	80	90	1600	10	20	30	40	50	60	70	80	90	1700	10

KEY: E= Edward M= Mary J= James II P= Reginald Pole G = Edmund Grindal B= Richard Bancroft . *(Note that from 1660 to 1663 William Juxton was archbishop, not shown above)*

= Reformers. = Early Leading Puritans = Later Well-known Puritans

Nicholas Ridley and Thomas Cranmer, I have chosen to describe John Bradford and John Hooper since they are in an especial sense prototypes of what was to follow. John Bradford was the first Englishman to expound in detail on the nature of evangelical repentance. Bishop John Hooper was outstanding in his pastoral concern for the parishes over which he had oversight. The ignorant state of the clergy at that time highlights the changes that were eventually to be achieved. Hooper was a man aflame with zeal for God and amazingly energetic in his labours for his people. This makes it all the more incredible that a leader of such quality should be condemned to burn at the stake.

The saying that 'The blood of the martyrs is the seed of the church' is true of the Puritans. When Mary came to the throne she was determined to return England to Rome. Superstitious, devious and unfaithful to her promises, she persecuted relentlessly all who stood in her way. Before her enthronement she promised a group of stalwart believers in Suffolk that religion would remain as it had been under her brother Edward. When she began to renege on her promise a delegation was sent from Suffolk to plead with her. The outcome was that she accused the leader of defamation and ordered that his ears be cut off! It is little wonder that, anticipating cruel persecution, 800 Protestants fled to the Continent.

The gruesome scenes of human bodies burning in public places were etched into the minds of the people, bringing about a deep detestation of the superstition and cruelty of Roman Catholicism. The faith, constancy and courage of those who died were the talk of the nation. We have seen the remarkable life of John Foxe and the crucial role he fulfilled in recording the details of the lives and deaths of these martyrs in his *Book of Martyrs* which had such an effect on the nation.

All these martyrs bore a glorious testimony. John Bradford and John Hooper especially exemplify characteristics which were typical of the Puritanism which was to develop. They and the other martyrs provided the bedrock upon which Puritanism was built.

John Bradford (1510-1555)

Bradford was born in Manchester of wealthy parents who sent him into the army for experience. He decided to follow law but in 1547 was dramatically converted through the testimony of a friend, Thomas Sampson, who later became an exile during Mary's reign. Bradford sold some valuable possessions, gave the proceeds to the poor and began to train for the ministry at Cambridge. He advanced rapidly in godliness. While at Cambridge he was influenced by the famous continental Reformer, Martin Bucer, who was teaching there at that time.

Bradford was ordained in 1550. Under the young King Edward, he was chosen to be one of six travelling chaplains preaching the gospel and teaching the doctrines of the Reformation. He was a powerful preacher. Foxe wrote of him: 'Sharply he opened and impugned sin, sweetly he preached Christ crucified, pithily he reproved heresies and errors, earnestly he persuaded the godly life.'

Bradford was cogent with his pen. Having preached often on repentance, he also wrote on it. It was the first written exposition in England on that central subject. Bradford inspired the Puritan emphasis

John Bradford

John Bradford (1510–1555)
In his devotional life, his emphasis on personal repentance and his outstanding work of encouraging fellow ministers, Bradford was a prototype of the Puritan — an example of the ministers to come.

on repentance. He was a pioneer in the Puritan practice of constancy in prayer: prayer upon rising, prayer before and after meals, before work and before retiring at night. Bradford was also an example in the art of maintaining piety by way of daily turning from sin and keeping a written spiritual diary of daily devotion.

Bradford's correspondence reveals him to have been a leader of exceptional spiritual calibre. His letters show us how the leading Christians of that time encouraged each other. Also in Bradford's letters we have a preview of what was to come in the bonding together of the Puritan pastors during the reign of Elizabeth.

With John Bradford, when he was burned at the stake in 1555, was a young apprentice aged nineteen named John Leaf. As they died together Bradford encouraged this young martyr with the words: 'Be of good comfort, brother: we shall have a merry supper with the Lord this night!'

John Hooper (1495-1555)

John Hooper, the only son of wealthy parents, was born in Somerset in 1495. He studied at Merton College, Oxford. On leaving he became a monk in the Cistercian order which stressed poverty, simplicity and solitude. On the dissolution of the monasteries he went first to London and then returned to Oxford. Being a diligent student of the Scriptures, especially of Paul's letters, he came to see the errors of Rome and became an ardent advocate of the Reformation. He had to leave England in 1546 and spent time at Strasbourg and Zurich. During his stay on the Continent, Hooper fully imbibed the spirit of the Reformation. John a Lasco (also known as Jan Laski, 1499-1560), son of one of the richest aristocratic families in Poland, was his closest friend. Lasco pastored a church made up of foreigners in London during the reign of Edward. This church was thoroughly reformed in character and had a powerful influence on Hooper's thinking.

Hooper returned to England after the death of Henry VIII. In 1551 he became Bishop of Gloucester. Controversy, requiring some compromise, surrounded his ordination because of his refusal to follow an order of service which contradicted his principles. Hooper was an excellent, powerful and popular preacher. Large crowds came to hear him. He was deeply exercised about the ignorance and corruption of the clergy and made it his habit to tour his diocese visiting the ministers.

One of his efforts aimed at local reformation was to send out a questionnaire to the 311 clergy of his diocese. Nine basic questions included: 'How many commandments are there? Where are they to be found? Can you show where the Lord's Prayer is found? Who is the author of the Lord's Prayer?' Nine did not know how many commandments there were; thirty-nine did not know the location of the Lord's Prayer and thirty-four did not know who the author was! Eight could not answer any of the questions. Such was the state of the clergy of the Church of England! This is important because it highlights vividly the change that was to come about from biblical illiteracy to England's being 'the land of the Bible'.

Hooper could be regarded as the first of the Puritans on account of his evangelistic and pastoral passion, his zeal to reform the church and his resistance of everything without a warrant from Scripture, such as the wearing of vestments. Hooper's life, example and martyrdom made a huge impact on England. He was a powerful influence on the Puritan movement.

John Hooper

John Hooper (1495–1555), Bishop of Gloucester, was burned at the stake. His outstanding example as a preacher, pastor and Reformer set an example which inspired generations to come. Like Bradford, his fellow-martyr, he typified the Puritans who followed in the next three generations.

The first generation of Puritans

If we take the lives of the Puritans of Elizabeth's reign as being the first generation, the second can be regarded as those who followed in the first half of the seventeenth century but who did not live up to the time of the Great Ejection in 1662. The principal event of this period was the Westminster Assembly (1643-47). The third generation can be taken as those who lived through the Ejection and beyond. It was in the latter period that most of the 'writing' Puritans (i.e. those whose works have been republished) lived.

As we saw in the story of the Puritans, a spiritual brotherhood developed in the 1580s and 1590s which was to provide the seedbed of the next generation of godly pastors. In that section I described the lives of Richard Greenham, Richard Rogers, Laurence Chaderton and William Perkins. The godly influence of these leaders formed a foundation for the future. Today we do well to ask if the next generation of ministers will be well grounded and powerful in the main principles of the Christian faith. We have already seen how Richard Greenham trained young men in the village of Dry Drayton in his 'School of Christ' and William Perkins influenced many young men at Cambridge. Perkins' books were very popular and largely shaped the thinking of the next generation of preachers. We remember too Laurence Chaderton and his long ministry at Cambridge. When he came to retire, forty people who had been converted through him came begging him to continue his ministry. We saw too the influence of Richard Rogers of Wethersfield, who was deeply exercised about the necessity and development of vital godliness as applied to every area of life.

We start with the short life of Edward Dering, which illustrates the Puritans' battle to reform the church, a work in which they did not succeed. We also look briefly at the life of Henry Smith, who resembled Dering in the quality of his preaching.

Then follows John Dod, who reminds us of the main ingredients of the spiritual lives of the brotherhood. Dod was an outstanding leader. He lived long and exercised a wide and pervasive influence as a powerful preacher, a godly pastor and an example of what it is to use hospitality to advance the cause of Christ. An often forgotten mark of an elder is that he must be hospitable. In this Dod excelled.

Next we look at Arthur Hildersam who was a great encouragement to his brother pastors. It is important to note that his life reflects the major shift away from Roman Catholicism that was taking place throughout this period. He was disinherited and even though he was connected in background to the royal family, he suffered much for his testimony. Some enjoyed protection on account of rich, sympathetic and aristocratic patrons. Hildersam did not.

Finally there is John Rogers. Every time I think of Rogers I think of the necessity of life and power in preaching. There are some preachers you will never and can never forget. Holy Spirit-anointed preaching is the need of this hour. In John Rogers' day there were those who travelled a long way to Dedham to hear him preach. They said that they went 'to fetch fire' at Dedham. Preachers today need 'to fetch fire' from heaven so that our preaching will be alive and convey life to our hearers.

Edward Dering (1540-1576)

Edward Dering was born into a distinguished family in Kent. In 1572 Dering married Anne Locke, a wealthy widow who admired the preaching of John Knox and had spent time in Geneva. The Puritan scholar Patrick Collinson calls Dering 'the archetype of the Puritan Divine, whose life and works were a model for many who would come after him in the 17th century' and 'an incomparable illustration of some of the more positive qualities of the Puritan spirit'.

Dering studied at Christ's College, Cambridge, early in Mary's reign, at which time Cambridge was a seedbed of Puritan religion. By the manner in which he wrote to his brothers we can tell that he was fervent in his evangelical faith. His main passion was the question of salvation from sin, how through a true faith in Christ we can be sure that we shall be saved in the great Day of Judgement and how the believer can be assured of his standing before a holy God.

Dering was esteemed as one of the outstanding Greek scholars of his time. He was chosen to make a Greek oration on the occasion of Queen Elizabeth's visit to the university

Edward Dering

in 1564. He was privileged in his friendship with the archbishop and enjoyed opportunities to preach on important occasions. There came a kind of mysterious watershed in his career in 1570 when Dering became indignant about the debased state of the ministry in the country. According to his friends he expressed this indignation too forcibly in his preaching.

In a sermon preached before the queen in her chapel on 25 February 1570 he reproved Her Majesty for neglect in her duty to rid the churches of unworthy incumbents, some of whom he described as 'ruffians, hawkers and dicers'. He pictured these ministers as blind guides and dumb dogs that will not bark. 'And yet you', he told her to her face, 'in the meanwhile that all

In a sermon preached before Queen Elizabeth in her chapel on 25 February 1570 Edward Dering reproved Her Majesty for neglect in her duty to rid the churches of unworthy incumbents, some of whom he described as 'ruffians, hawkers and dicers'. He pictured these ministers as blind guides and dumb dogs that will not bark. 'And yet you', he told her to her face, 'in the meanwhile that all these whoredoms are committed, you at whose hands God will require it, you sit still and are careless, and let men do as they will.'

these whoredoms are committed, you at whose hands God will require it, you sit still and are careless, and let men do as they will.' Unlike Whitgift (later to be promoted to archbishop) who used his opportunity to preach before the queen to impress her, Dering seemed impervious to the consequences of reminding her that great power involved commensurate responsibility. Perhaps Dering was free of the temptation of ambition and self-interest as he sensed that he would not live long because of tuberculosis. That disease was in fact to take him to an early grave. No Elizabethan sermon was more reprinted than Dering's remarkable oration in which he confronted the queen with her responsibilities.

Courageous preaching of this kind, which exposed the dreadful spiritual state of the clergy, embarrassed Parker, the Archbishop of Canterbury, and Cecil, Elizabeth's first minister. It is not surprising that Dering's influence declined. However, he continued to enjoy the confidence of Sandys, Bishop of London, who gave him the privilege of preaching in St Paul's, London. There Dering preached an outstanding and powerful series of sermons on Hebrews which accorded him the reputation of being the greatest preacher of his day.

In 1570 to 1572 controversy about church government raged, fuelled by the writings of Cartwright, Field and Wilcox. Dering was called to declare where he stood in relationship to these writings. Unlike Perkins, Dering was not a systematic theologian and was fairly ambivalent about church government. His enemies were determined to have him removed from privilege and office. However, Dering was so well connected and protected by men of high rank that it was difficult to suspend him. Efforts to silence him all failed. Queen Elizabeth ordered that Dering not only be silenced but removed from his lectureship. Even that failed as her deputies could not agree among themselves as to the formulation of the charge to be brought against him.

Letter-writing formed an important part of Dering's ministry. This included letters of spiritual counsel to women of high standing and influence. It is a feature of the Puritan movement that often the most enthusiastic supporters of Puritan ministries were women, some of whom were deeply committed to reformation whereas their husbands were less so. One of Dering's correspondents was Mrs Honywood, a lady who was plagued about her assurance of salvation. Mrs Honywood once told John Foxe that she was as surely damned as this glass which she held in her hand. She then hurled the glass violently to the floor. Amazingly the glass bounced up without any damage!

When dying aged thirty-six Dering was surrounded by fellow-preachers who wrote down his last words. He left this world having made a wonderful contribution to the Puritan movement.

Henry Smith (1560-1591)

Dering in his direct style and passionate preaching was similar to Henry Smith whose ministry made its impact in London in the following decade. Smith, a student of William Greenhill, was called to St Clement Danes, London, where capacity crowds — grocers, locksmiths, tradesmen, people of every sort — flocked to hear him. He was a wonderful preacher and was nicknamed 'the silver-tongued Smith'. Such was his power in preaching that he could hold the hearts of his hearers in his hands and steer them wherever he pleased — and he was pleased to steer them only to God's glory and their own good. He was proficient in the business of redemption. He died aged only thirty-one but, like Edward Dering, 'he lived long in a little time'.

John Dod (1550-1645)

Born in Cheshire, John Dod went to Cambridge to study at Jesus College. While he was 'in his natural state of sin' he flew into such a temper when accused of not paying the college steward that he was overcome with a fever. It is reported that it was then that 'His sins came upon him like an armed man, and the tide of his thoughts was turned.' His conversion was real and new life began. An interesting record shows that the steward remembered that he had, after all, been paid.

Dod was much in demand as a popular preacher. He settled for twenty years at Hanwell in Oxfordshire, where he exercised a powerful preaching ministry which was instrumental in the conversion of hundreds of souls. With four other preachers he set up a lectureship at Banbury. Like Hildersam, he experienced fierce persecution from 1604 onwards.

William Haller, in his book *The Rise of Puritanism*, describes Dod as the chief holy man of the spiritual brotherhood and says of him, 'He had the English gift of humour and the knack of salty speech.' Cartwright describes Dod as being 'the fittest man in the land for a pastoral function, able to speak to any man's capacity'. According to one of his disciples, 'All his discourses were sermons and that with such a mixture of delight, as would take any man; so facetious and pithy that, if all his sayings were collected, they would exceed all that Plutarch in Greek or others in Latin have published.' And another reported, 'Poor simple people that never knew what religion meant, when they had gone to hear him, could not but choose to talk of his sermon. It mightily affected poor creatures to hear the mysteries of God brought down to their language and dialect.' One of Dod's sayings was that he would rather preach an old sermon ten times than speak any new thing without preparation.

John Dod preached twice on Sunday and once during the week. After every sermon his wife opened the house to all comers. We read of him, 'He brought in many to dinner including four to six widows who helped him as deaconesses would. If his wife began to doubt that there would be enough food to go round he would respond, "Better want meat than good company, but there is something in this house even though cold." Eating little himself but bidding the rest fall to, he would go on talking. He had plenty to say, and when he was faint he would call for a small glass of wine mixed with beer, and then talk again till night.'

Many looked to Dod for wisdom. Two well-known Puritans, Job Throckmorton and John Preston, both seeing in the same year that their lives were drawing to a close, settled in Dod's area in order to have the advantage of his spiritual counsel. Unusually for a Puritan minister, Job Throckmorton experienced a major problem concerning his personal assurance of salvation. Shortly before he died he asked Mr Dod, 'What will you say of him who is going out of this world, and can find no comfort?' 'What will you say of our Saviour Christ,' replied Dod, 'who when he was going out of the world found no comfort but cried, "My God, My God, why hast thou forsaken me?"' This administered comfort to Throckmorton's troubled soul and when he died soon afterwards he was rejoicing in the Lord.

Since Dod lived to the age of ninety-five, it is not surprising to discover that, in addition to his own pastoral work, he was a counsellor to those who had to weigh up the factors about leaving England to cross the Atlantic for a new life in America.

Arthur Hildersam (1563-1631)

Hildersam was related to the royal family. His parents were Roman Catholic. Steeped in the doctrines of Rome, he was taught to repeat his prayers in Latin. He chose to study at Cambridge, where he was converted. His father was furious and determined to send him to Rome for reclamation. Arthur refused and was disinherited. However one of his wide circle of wealthy relatives, the Earl of Huntingdon, who sympathized with his dilemma, sent him back to Cambridge endowed with generous support.

In 1588 Hildersam was charged with the offence of preaching before he was officially ordained. He was ordered to make a public confession of repentance. A statement in abject penitent style survives as a printed document but there is doubt as to whether Hildersam ever read this out in a public apology.

It was while under the shadows of this public reproach that he was called to Ashby-de-la-Zouch in Leicestershire where he continued to the end of his life, a period of forty-three years. During that time he often suffered persecution. The influence of his preaching was profound and widespread but it also stirred, in those who rejected his message, the most virulent hatred towards him. When King James came to power Hildersam was esteemed one of the foremost leaders of the Puritans and was appointed as a representative to present the Millenary Petition signed by over 1,000 clergy. This petition pleaded for reformation.

In 1590 he married and this union was greatly blessed. His wife proved to be a constant comfort and strength in the persecutions which he suffered.

During his subsequent ministry he suffered several periods of being silenced. For instance, in 1616 he was excommunicated, degraded from the ministry and ordered to be thrown into prison for not submitting to the rites of the Church of England. At the same time he was fined the outrageous sum of £2,000, a vast sum of money in those days which was entirely beyond his means.

Hildersam was not guilty of drunkenness or adultery or any such immorality. It was only due to his refusal to conform to the rites and ceremonies of the Church of England that he suffered these extreme penalties. He was resented on account of his very widespread spiritual influence and was dubbed 'a *ringleader* of all schismatical persons in that part of the country'.

The manner in which he faced this trial which threatened to destroy him is instructive inasmuch as it reminds us that when we face extraordinary problems we must persevere in prayer and deal with each factor one by one. Prayerfully Arthur set about extricating himself step by step. The first move was to get out of prison. This was by appeal to influential friends. The previous year, when he was in prison on a similar charge of refusing to conform, a friend had written to Archbishop Abbot, who had responded with impatience saying that Hildersam would die in prison if he did not conform. He was released but still had to face the fine, which was completely beyond his ability to pay. He wrote to a Lady Fielding asking that she use her influence to have the fine reduced. He wrote to the Earl of Suffolk along similar lines seeking his help. Eventually the fine was reduced but he still had to pay an exorbitant sum of money.

During his last illness Hildersam was noted for his spiritual, holy and heavenly conversation. To his son he gave a solemn charge to take heed to the flock. It was while he was praying with his son that he entered upon the joy of his Lord.

In his *Lives of the Puritans* Benjamin Brook devotes twelve pages to Hildersam. He was outstanding in the attribute of meekness. He was not flamboyant or aggressive in his nonconformity, but firm and patient. The quality of his humility is seen in one of his statements that he always sought to benefit from the preaching of others. He declared that he never failed to be edified by faithful preaching even when the preacher was not endowed with natural talent.

Among the admirers of Arthur Hildersam were William Gouge, John Preston and John Cotton. His disciples saw in their ideal spiritual physician one who was always willing 'to instruct the ignorant, to satisfy the doubtful, to settle the wavering, to comfort the dejected, and to encourage all sorts in the exercises of religion'.[1] We see exemplified in

Hildersam the advantages of spending a lifetime in one pastorate, enduring and surviving enormous opposition and many distractions, but always remaining patient and steadfast, a wonderful example of godliness. He did not leave behind any literature apart from two substantial expositions, one on John chapter 4 and the other on Psalm 51.

John Rogers (1566-1636)

John Rogers of Dedham, Essex, was a near relative of Richard Rogers of Wethersfield in Essex, whose life we have already looked at in our overview of the period. Richard supported John Rogers in his studies at Cambridge and persevered with him even though he was so given to sin that he sold his books to follow his pleasure-loving, worldly habits. Eventually John provoked Richard Rogers to the point of giving him up but Richard's wife persuaded him to try once more, which reminds us of the parable of the fig-tree: '"For three years now I've been coming to look for fruit on this fig-tree and haven't found any. Cut it down! Why should it use up the soil?" "Sir," the man replied, "leave it alone for one more year, and I'll dig round it and fertilize it. If it bears fruit next year, fine! If not, then cut it down"' (Luke 13:7-8). This persevering concern of Mrs Richard Rogers was rewarded, for John was converted and in due course became one of the most powerful of all the Puritan preachers.

John Rogers

John Rogers (d. 1636)

John Rogers was regarded as one of the most awakening preachers of his age. Many souls were converted through his preaching. Believers would travel many miles to 'to fetch fire from Dedham', Dedham being the town where he ministered. 'To fetch fire' is unusually expressive. It points to the need of spiritual vitality and reminds us of how the Holy Spirit imparts spiritual vitality through powerful preaching.

The gift of preaching was given to John Rogers in such a marked way that it was said of him that few heard him preach without trembling. Many souls were converted through his preaching and he was regarded as one of the most awakening preachers of his age. Bishop Brownrigg used to say, 'John Rogers will do more good with his wild notes, than we [bishops] with our set music!' People crowded to hear him from a wide area. Often many were disappointed at not being able to gain admittance. A well-known Puritan minister, Giles Firmin, records that he owed his conversion to the first sentences he ever heard from John Rogers. Some young men went to hear him preach and although they were late managed to squeeze in. Seeing them come in, John Rogers cried out, 'Here are some young ones come for Christ. Will nothing serve you but you must have Christ? Then you shall have him!' Giles Firmin was gripped at once and converted.

John Rogers' power in preaching is illustrated by an occasion when the famous Puritan Thomas Goodwin (then a young man) was reduced under his preaching to helpless tears of repentance and gratitude towards God. Goodwin himself told the story to the renowned John Howe years later. Howe recalls the incident: 'Mr Rogers was ... on the subject of the Scriptures. And in that sermon he falls into an expostulation with the people about their neglect of the Bible... He personates God to the people telling them, "Well, I have trusted you so long with my Bible: you have slighted it; it lies in such and such a house all covered with dust and cobwebs. You care not to look at it. Do you use my Bible so? Well, you shall have my Bible no longer." And he takes up the Bible from his cushion and seemed as if he were going away with it and carrying it from them; but immediately [he] turns again and impersonates the people to God, falls down on his knees, cries and pleads most earnestly, "Lord, whatsoever thou dost to us take not the Bible from us; kill our children, burn our houses, destroy our goods; only spare us thy Bible, take not away thy Bible." And then he personates God again to the people, "Say you so? Well, I will try you a little while longer; and here is my Bible for you; I will see how you use it, whether you will love it more, whether you will practise it more and live more according to it."' Howe continues to recall the effect of all this: 'By these actions (as the Doctor told me) he put the congregation into so strange a posture that he never saw any congregation in, in his life; the place was a mere Bochim, the people generally (as it were) deluged with their own tears; and he told me that he himself when he got out and was to take horse again was fain to hang a quarter of an hour on the neck of his horse weeping, before he had the power to mount, so strange an impression was there upon him and generally upon the people having been thus expostulated with for neglect of the Bible.'

The greatest need of our times is the recovery of true Holy Spirit unction in preaching the gospel to the saving of sinners. The fervour, power and expressiveness of John Rogers in the pulpit was typical of the Puritans.

The second generation

In the 'Story of the Puritans' I described the events leading up to the Civil War. It was during that time, on 12 June 1643, that Parliament passed an ordinance calling for 'an Assembly of learned and godly divines for the settling of the Government and Liturgy of the Church of England'. On 1 July the Westminster Assembly convened.

The Confession of Faith and *Catechisms* that were drawn up by them and endorsed by Parliament have had a profound effect on subsequent church history. Whole books have been devoted to a description of the Westminster Assembly. Those ministers involved needed to be within reasonable travelling distance of London in order meaningfully to attend the sessions and debates of the assembly. Of the five ministers that I describe now, Robert Harris, Jeremiah Burroughs and William Gouge were members of the assembly. Richard Sibbes, a very well-known Puritan on account of his writings, died in 1635. Robert Bolton was known especially as a physician of the soul. He was typical of the Puritans who during this phase of history were multiplying — a multiplication which can be seen in the number of outstanding ministers available to participate in the Westminster Assembly.

Robert Bolton

Robert Bolton (1572-1631) wrote Instructions for a Right Comforting of Afflicted Consciences based on lectures he gave at Kettering. The work is pastoral and practical in character and reflects the high profile given to the role of conscience among the Puritans. This famous 390-page work by Bolton has been republished by Soli Deo Gloria.

Robert Bolton (1572-1631)

Robert Bolton was a well-known Puritan and his fame continues today mainly because of the republication of his best-known work, *A Treatise on Comforting Afflicted Consciences,* first published in 1626. John MacArthur Jr says of this book, 'It remains a definitive study in how to deal practically with guilt.' Writing in the foreword of the 1991 *Soli Deo Gloria* reprint, MacArthur points out that he does not know of a single book published in the previous twenty years that explains in depth how to respond biblically to a grieved or wounded conscience! Other books of quality by Bolton are *A Comfortable Walking with God,* and *Four Last Things: Death, Judgement, Hell and Heaven.*[2]

Robert Bolton was born in Blackburn in Lancashire in 1572. His parents observed that he was exceptionally gifted. They were poor but they sacrificed financially for him to be well educated. In grammar school he attained the status of best scholar. At the age of twenty he went to Lincoln College, Oxford, where he proved to be an outstanding student. He mastered the Greek language and such was his ability that he was able to support himself as a teacher until he became a tutor in the university at the age of thirty.

In all this time he was not converted. Indeed he loved this present evil world and was hostile to the ministry of godly preachers like William Perkins, the well-known Puritan teacher at Cambridge. However, Bolton came under deep conviction of sin. This lasted for several months and was so intense and painful that his experience has been compared to that of Martin Luther. Eventually he came into peace through faith in Christ and trusted only in that righteousness which is the gift of God. Aged thirty-five, he was ordained into the Christian ministry. When he was forty he married and was wonderfully blessed in his wife, who enthusiastically supported him in his ministry. Bolton was outstanding in the quality and energy of his labours. It is said of him that his entire aim in preaching was to convert his hearers and under God's blessing hundreds were savingly converted. He spent twenty years in a vigorous ministry in the parish of Broughton in Northamptonshire.

Having been a slave of worldly pleasures, he knew at first hand how to expose sin in all its deceptive, destructive and poisoning powers. Bolton was bold and uncompromising in his style of preaching and prepared by rehearsing his sermons to himself in private before preaching them in public. Like John the Baptist and our Lord, he was fearless and had no regard for the hatred and resentment that can be aroused through a faithful ministry. It was noted that he was thoroughly at ease in preaching the free and full offer of the gospel to all without exception. He was wholly committed to a life of prayer and made it his habit to pray six times in the day. He also observed special days for humiliation and prayer, especially before leading the Lord's Supper.

In his last illness, at the age of sixty, Bolton bore a glorious testimony to his people and family. He fervently prayed for them all and was very direct with them personally about salvation, commending each in prayer to the Lord. He was full of personal assurance of his acceptance with God and expressed his great longing to depart and be with Christ, which is far better.

Robert Harris (1578-1658)

Born at Broad Camden in Gloucestershire, Robert Harris went to school at Chipping Camden, then to Worcester and from there to Magdalen Hall, Oxford, where he was taught by Goffe, who was a Puritan. Harris was not a believer but bought a Bible and some theological books which led to his conversion. With his tutor he studied Greek, Hebrew and Calvin's *Institutes*.

He was invited to preach at Chipping Camden. Such was the ignorance in that area that no Bible could be found to use in the pulpit. The clergyman had lost his Bible! A search was made and eventually the lost Bible was found. Harris then preached from Romans 10:1: 'Brothers, my heart's desire and prayer to God for Israel is that they may be saved.' At that time Harris persuaded his father to support him further in his studies at Oxford. Not long afterwards an epidemic of the plague broke out. In those days the plague could destroy more than half of the population.

Harris found lodgings about five miles from Oxford where opportunities to preach opened to him. 1604-1605 was a period of severe persecution. About 300 ministers were suspended from office. Among these was John Dod, who at that time was minister of Hanwell. The outstanding talents and learning of Robert Harris constrained the bishop in charge of Hanwell to agree to his being ordained there. About this time he married. Also at that time a close friendship developed between John Dod and Harris. Here we have an example of the way in which the Puritans strengthened each other in unity and vision for the gospel and for reformation.

Harris continued to minister in Hanwell for about forty years. As many used to come to John Dod for spiritual counsel, so likewise many young preachers sought the wisdom and leadership of Robert Harris. He was blessed with many children and all of them followed in the pathway of righteousness and honoured Christ in their callings. Harris was very disciplined in his lifestyle. Of liquor he said he would rather pour it into his boots than into his mouth between meals! He allowed himself half of Saturday for physical recreation. He observed that the most humble preachers were instrumental in converting souls rather than the greatest scholars who were proud. Nevertheless he himself worked hard in his study, and his scholarship and preaching ministry were much valued by the whole university fraternity in Oxford. His gifts were recognized in London and he was frequently invited to preach before Parliament and participated in the work of the Westminster Assembly.

In 1644 at the onset of the Civil War he lost all his possessions in the upheaval. A company of soldiers strongly opposed to Harris were living in the town. Their evil language constrained him to preach a sermon on James 5:12: 'Swear not at all!' This so offended the soldiers that they swore they would shoot him if he preached again from the same text. Undismayed by their threats, he did just that the following Lord's Day. As he was preaching he noticed a soldier preparing his weapon as if to shoot. Not perturbed, Harris completed his sermon.

In his last illness Robert Harris testified, 'I never in all my life saw the worth of Christ, nor tasted the sweetness of God's love in that measure as now I do.'

Richard Sibbes (1577-1635)

Richard Sibbes was educated at St John's College, Cambridge. He was called to be a lecturer at Trinity College where his preaching was instrumental in the conversion of many. John Cotton, afterwards to become a famous leader in New England, was one of the students converted under his ministry. His reputation as a preacher and teacher spread and this led to a regular ministry in London at Gray's Inn. Gray's Inn was then, as now, one of the most important centres for legal study and practice. Benjamin Brook says that 'Besides the learned lawyers, many of the nobility and gentry, as well as citizens, flocked to hear him; and great numbers had abundant cause to bless God for the benefit which they derived from his ministry.' He was careful always to lay a good foundation in the heads and hearts of his hearers. In private life he was charitable to the poor and an excellent pastor.

In 1626 Sibbes became master of St Catherine's College. The terms of his ministry in London required that he should hold no other ecclesiastical living, but since he had an assistant at Gray's Inn, and since he never married, it was practical for him to travel to Cambridge during the week. St Catherine's had passed through a long period of decline when Sibbes took up the mastership. Finance was at a low ebb and there were few students. Sibbes was used to turn this situation round and lead the college into the most brilliant period of its history.

Sibbes' influence in Cambridge as a *pastor pastorum*, a maker and shaper of ministers, was second only to that of William Perkins. His preaching in the same church where Perkins had ministered, St Mary's, had widespread influence, as did his ministry at Gray's Inn in London.

Inasmuch as Richard Sibbes was a physician of the heart who expounded the soul's conflict, he anticipates the ministry a century later of Jonathan Edwards (1703-1758) and his most famous book, *The Religious Affections*. The best-known books by Sibbes are *The Bruised Reed and The Smoking Flax, The Returning Backslider* and *The Soul's Conflict*. Sibbes is one of the best-known Puritans and his influence pervaded every part of the Puritan movement.

Richard Sibbes

(1577-1635).

Richard Sibbes was a physician of the soul, which is reflected in his expositions, 'The Bruised Reed and smoking Flax', 'The Returning Backslider' and 'The Soul's Conflict'. Sibbes is one of the best-known Puritans and his influence pervaded the Puritan movement.

THE
EIGHTH BOOK
OF
Mr Jeremiah Burroughs.
Being a Treatise of the
EVIL of EVILS,
OR THE
Exceeding Sinfulness
OF
SIN.

Wherein is shewed,
1 There is more Evil in the least Sin, than there is in the greatest Affliction.
2 Sin is most opposite to God.
3 Sin is most opposite to Mans Good.
4 Sin is opposite to all Good in general.
5 Sin is the Poyson, or Evil of all other Evils.
6 Sin hath a kind of Infiniteness in it.
7 Sin makes a man conformable to the Devil.
All these several Heads are branched out into very many Particulars.

Published by
Thomas Goodwyn, William Bridge, Sydrach Sympson, William Adderly, William Greenhil, Philip Nye, John Yates.

London, Printed by Peter Cole in Leaden-Hall, and are to be sold at his Shop at the Sign of the Printing-Press in Cornhil, neer the Royal Exchange. 1654.

Jeremiah Burroughs (1599-1646)

Burroughs is described by Benjamin Brook in his three-volume work, *The Lives of the Puritans*, as 'a very amiable divine' (i.e. theologian) who was educated at Emmanuel College, Cambridge, but quit the university and afterwards England on account of his non-conformity. He assisted Edmund Calamy at St Edmunds and then enjoyed a five-year lectureship in Tivetshall, Norfolk. When persecution increased he was deprived of his living and in 1636 fled to Holland where he assisted William Bridge, who was pastor of a church in Rotterdam.

Jeremiah Burroughs (1599-1646)
Burroughs was an exceptionally fine preacher and wrote as well as he preached. He was a prolific worker and wrote extensively, but always with quality, penetration and spirituality. It is quite remarkable that at the time of his death, at the early age of forty-seven, he left so much writing of enduring quality.

With the commencement of the Civil War the power of the bishops to persecute subsided. Burroughs then returned to England, where he ministered to the London congregations of Cripplegate and Stepney, which were reputed to have the largest attendances in England. He took the 7.00 a.m. service at Stepney and William Greenhill preached at 3.00 p.m. The saying spread that Burroughs was the morning star and Greenhill the evening star of Stepney.

Burroughs was chosen to be one of the delegates to take part in the Westminster Assembly. He was a man of peace. Richard Baxter, who knew his virtues well, maintained that 'If all the Episcopalians had been like Archbishop Ussher; all the Presbyterians like Mr Stephen Marshall; and all the Independents like Mr Jeremiah Burroughs; the breaches of the church would soon have been healed.'

Burroughs was an exceptionally fine preacher and wrote as well as he preached. He was a prolific worker and his extensive writings were consistently penetrating and spiritual. It is quite remarkable that at the time of his death, at the age of only forty-seven, he left so much writing of enduring quality. His most popular work is *The Rare Jewel of Christian Contentment*.[3] A number of his writings have been republished in recent years, including *A Treatise on the Evil of Evils* (a study on sin), *The Excellency of a Gracious Spirit, A Treatise on Earthly-Mindedness, Gospel Worship, Gospel Fear, Gospel Remission, Gospel Conversation, The Saints' Happiness* (The Beatitudes), and *The Saints' Treasury.*[4]

Burroughs' treatise of about 400 pages on peace is as relevant today as the time it was written. Its title is: *Irenicum, to Lovers of Truth and Peace. Heart-divisions opened, in the causes and evils of them; With cautions that we may be hurt by them, and endeavours to heal them.* Of Burroughs' four-volume work on Hosea Spurgeon declared: 'Masterly. A vast treasure house of experimental exposition.'[5]

William Gouge (1575-1653)

Born at Bow in Middlesex, William Gouge was educated at Eton School and then St Catherine's College, Cambridge. He was blessed with a fine intellect and was exceedingly disciplined in study. In nine years he was never absent from college prayers at 5.30 a.m. unless sick. He made it his

William Gouge

habit to read fifteen chapters of the Bible a day. At college he was chosen as reader of logic and philosophy. Those who were envious nicknamed him the 'arch-Puritan'.

In 1608 he was chosen as minister of Blackfriars Church, London. There he ministered for forty-six years until his death in 1653. He received many offers of ministerial appointments in other churches but he used to say, 'It is my highest ambition to go from Blackfriars to heaven!' For thirty-five years Gouge maintained a Wednesday morning lecture. Benjamin Brook writes of Gouge, 'So great was his fame, that when religious persons from distant parts of the country

William Gouge (1575–1653).
For forty-five years William Gouge preached effectually with a soul-saving ministry to one of the largest congregations in London. For thirty-three years he preached through the epistle to the Hebrews. The substance of this preaching shows a skilful balance of doctrine experience and practical application. He received many offers of ministerial appointments in other churches, but he used to say, 'It is my highest ambition to go from Blackfriars to heaven!' It is recorded that thousands were converted and built up under his ministry.

went to London, they did not think their business finished, unless they had attended a Blackfriars lecture. The success of his ministry was also very great. It is said that thousands were converted and built up under his ministry.' Assessment of conversion was quite different in those days. A convert was one who demonstrated in his life that he was a new person in Christ. Today decisions are reported as though they were conversions. Sadly, very few decisions can be equated with true conversion.

Gouge was a peaceable man and described as being the very picture of Moses for a meek and quiet spirit. He was never observed by his family or by his servants to speak in anger to his wife. Yet in spite of his peaceable disposition he was thrown into prison for nine weeks, simply for republishing a book on the calling of the Jews. He was also persecuted for opposing the Arminianism and ritualism of Archbishop Laud.

An early riser throughout the year, Gouge was troubled if any persons should be at their work before he was at his. He was a fervent believer in the Lord's Day and made sure that his servants were able to have full profit from that day. He was deeply exercised about the welfare of overseas churches and would weep, fast and pray when he heard bad news of the suffering of believers in foreign countries.

William Gouge was a member of the Westminster Assembly and often filled the moderator's chair when that gentleman was absent. His most famous series of sermons was on the letter to the Hebrews, a work of 1,100 pages.

The third generation

It is evident that the Puritan movement reached its apex from about 1640 to 1660, after which the number of gifted ministers declined. This high point is seen in the quality of works written during these times and especially those by very well-known Puritans who are famous still. I will now provide brief biographies of the best-known, such as Goodwin, Bridge, Manton, Charnock, Owen, Baxter, Bunyan, Flavel and Howe, all of whose *Complete Works* have been republished since about 1965.

Thomas Watson is a favourite Puritan author on account of his easy-to-read, colourful style and pithiness in doctrinal definition. His writings have not been gathered into one uniform set. I have included details of his principal works because his books are descriptive of his ministry.

Bunyan, Owen and Baxter were the most famous of the Puritans. Jessey and Knollys, both Baptists, are less known. I have included them to illustrate the diversity of character that prevailed among these men. Jessey, out of devotion to his work, chose not to marry. He was exemplary in caring for the poor and in addition took measures to assist Jews in their practical needs. Knollys is included in my choice of lives not only because of the exceptional nature of his versatile ministry but because he was involved in both *The First* and *Second London Baptist Confessions of Faith.*

Dr Thomas Goodwin (1600-1679)

Thomas Goodwin has been accorded his doctorate of divinity here only to distinguish him from another notable Puritan of the same name who ministered in the county of Essex. Dr Thomas Goodwin had the advantage of godly parents who secured for him the best classical education in the neighbourhood so that before he reached his thirteenth birthday he entered Christ's College, Cambridge. At that time the whole of Cambridge was affected by the powerful ministry of William Perkins. Looking back on his experience Goodwin maintained that although he attended holy communion and was religious he was legalistic in spiritual matters and unconverted.

At the age of twenty, he experienced deep conviction of sin under a sermon on Jesus' tears over Jerusalem (Luke 19:41-42). He testified that the Holy Spirit directed his focus away from looking within to looking to Christ alone. This ended seven years of bondage for him. His own painful experience of conviction had much to do with his becoming a preacher who would be exceedingly useful in the conversion of sinners and the guidance of enquirers.

Following his conversion Goodwin allied himself to the Puritan party and in due course he followed Richard Sibbes as master of St Catherine's College, Cambridge. Persecution intensified at this time and he resigned his position in

Dr Thomas Goodwin

(1600-1679)

'For a generation to produce only one really great theologian in the Church's history is admirable. Yet the same generation that produced an Owen gave us also a Goodwin, who, with his majestic grasp of theology linked to a warm and visionary delight in the wonders of grace, stands as one of the greatest "experimental" theologians we have ever had' (Peter Lewis).

1634. We know that Goodwin settled for a while in Amsterdam, where he had fellowship with Nye, Burroughs, Bridge and Sympson. Later, at the Westminster Assembly, these men, being Independents rather than Presbyterians, became known as the 'dissenting brethren'. At the Assembly Nye was a powerful speaker, Burroughs an acute reasoner, Bridge a persuasive pleader, but Goodwin was the strength of the party. Such was the gracious and gentle character of Goodwin that even those who differed most from him regarded him with esteem. He was very close to Oliver Cromwell and ministered to him when Cromwell was dying.

In 1649 Goodwin was appointed president of Magdalen College, Oxford. He loved to assist young men in preparation for the ministry and, having been obliged to leave Cambridge in dark times, he confessed that he had not expected that he would ever recover such a position. With the restoration of the monarchy the political situation changed and in 1660 Goodwin moved to London where he ministered steadfastly even through 1665, the year of the plague. In the following year in the Great Fire he lost half his library in the flames. This was the occasion of his writing a wonderful work with the title *Patience and its perfect work under sudden and sore trials.* I well remember an unforgettable impression being made on the Whitefield Fraternal in Sussex in the 1960s. About forty ministers were deeply moved when Ferrell Griswold described the sufferings of Christ, his physical sufferings and his spiritual sufferings. Pastor Griswold, deeply read in the Puritans, ascribed the power of those expositions to the writings of Thomas Goodwin.

Goodwin's writing, like his preaching, is experimental in tone. He wrote as he felt. Highly commended in Goodwin's works is his experimental exposition entitled *The Return of Prayers*.

William Bridge (1600-1670)

Bridge was educated at Emmanuel College, Cambridge, where he began his studies at the age of sixteen. He was evidently gifted in academic work and became a fellow of the college, remaining there until the age of twenty-six. He ministered in Essex and then in Norwich as rector of St Peter's. It was there that he was silenced by Bishop Wren for his nonconformity and then excommunicated. This severe treatment drove him into exile and he took refuge in Holland, where he settled at Rotterdam. There he became pastor to the English church and was associated with Jeremiah Burroughs. He renounced the ordination which he had received in the Church of England and was re-ordained in the Independent style by Samuel Ward (1577-1639), a well-known Puritan from Suffolk who had suffered imprisonment for his faith.

William Bridge returned to England in 1642. He frequently preached before Parliament and was chosen as one of the members of the Westminster Assembly. He was called to be the minister of a church in Yarmouth, where he continued until ejected in 1662. His writings were gathered into five volumes in 1845 and republished in 1989. Like so many of the Puritans, he preached first and wrote down his material afterwards. His style is richly experimental and practical and often characterized by the most tender pastoral concern. This latter quality is seen especially in his most famous single piece of writing, *A Lifting up for the Downcast.*[6]

Thomas Manton (1620-1677)

Thomas Manton was privileged to have a father and both grandfathers as ministers. He was endued with much natural ability and was ready for university at the early age of fourteen, but his parents kept him at home for a further year before he entered Wadham College, Oxford. After basic studies he concentrated on theology. He was ordained to the ministry by the famous Joseph Hall, then Bishop of Exeter. After a three-year ministry in Devon he moved to a church in Stoke Newington, London, and seven years later took over from the aged Obadiah Sedgwick at Covent Garden, where he continued until his death in 1677.

Manton had a high esteem for Christopher Love (1618-1651), a young minister who was executed by beheading in 1651 for allegedly conspiring with the royalist cause. Manton attended Love on the scaffold. We can admire the courage of Manton in preaching the funeral sermon of Love even though soldiers threatened to shoot him. Manton suffered imprisonment during the post-1662 period.

While he was minister at Covent Garden many of high rank attended his ministry and he was called at times to

Thomas Manton
(1620-1677)

preach before Parliament. He became one of Oliver Cromwell's chaplains. An incident is on record which shows that the best men can fail at times. Manton was invited to preach before the Lord Mayor. He chose a difficult subject in which he could display his learning. For this the Lord rebuked him in the form of a poor man who reproached him later that day, complaining that he had come to get food for his soul but was greatly disappointed. Dr Manton was truly grieved and replied, 'Friend, if I did not give you a sermon, you have given me one; and by the grace of God I will never play the fool to preach before my Lord Mayor in such a manner again!'

Of the 130 sermons preached on Psalm 119 by Manton Spurgeon declared, 'There is not a poor discourse in the whole collection: he is evenly good, constantly excellent.' Spurgeon's verdict for what fills most of volumes 6-9 of his works is true of all twenty-two volumes. A truly exemplary expositor!

Thomas Manton was a zealous believer in family worship. He began morning and evening with a short prayer, then read a chapter from the Bible and required that his children and servants remember some part of it. He would then comment in an easy and pleasant style on what had been read, concluding with a longer prayer. He was ardent in the ministry on the Lord's Day, both in public worship and in his family, and was noted for the lively and affectionate way in which he administered the Lord's Supper. He rested on Mondays and received visitors.

In 1871 the complete twenty-two-volume set of Manton's writings was republished. As part of the introduction Bishop J. C. Ryle wrote an estimate of Manton in which he stated that 'The Puritans, as a body, have done more to elevate the national character than any class of Englishmen that ever lived.' A hundred years later, in the 1970s, a limited edition of 1,000 copies was published in the USA. Manton was only thirty when his commentary on James was published. His commentaries on 2 Thessalonians 2:1-12, James, Jude and Psalm 119 are particularly valuable.

Stephen Charnock (1628-1680)

Born in London, Stephen Charnock studied at Emmanuel College, Cambridge, where he experienced the saving change of salvation by grace. He took his first pastorate at Southwark in London.

Shortly after, aged only twenty-four, he was appointed to a senior position at New College, Oxford. This was followed by service in a high-ranking family in Dublin.

Difficult days lay ahead because the restoration of Charles II meant that Charnock was without a pastoral charge in London for fifteen years. He laboured for a short period in a Congregational church before his death at the age of fifty-two. Very little is known of his personal life. His title to fame lies in the excellence of his written works. The Banner of Truth has published three volumes of his discourses, including a wonderful series on the new birth. His most famous work is an extended series of expositions, in four volumes, on *The Existence and Attributes of God.*

Charnock's *Complete Works* were gathered and published in 1815 in 1866 and again in 1997 in five volumes.[7] The editor wrote, 'Holiness was the ornament of his life, usefulness the character of his ministry, the gospel he had so often preached the consolation of his dying hours.'

Stephen Charnock (1628–1680)

Charnock's title to fame lies in the excellence of his written works. The Banner of Truth have published three volumes of his discourses, including a powerful 226-page treatise on the subject of sin in which he shows that unbelief is the greatest sin. Highly commended in these reprinted volumes is Charnock's series of expositions on the new birth. His most famous writing is an extended series of expositions on the attributes of God.

Thomas Watson (*c.*1620-*c.*1686)

Thomas Watson's dates of birth and death are uncertain. It is estimated that he was born in 1620 and died in 1686. We do know that he graduated from Emmanuel College, Cambridge, with a Bachelor of Arts degree in 1639 and a Master's degree in 1642. He was recognized as an excellent student. In 1646 he became the rector of St Stephen's in the ward of Walbrook, London. He was implicated in

Thomas Watson

(1620–1686)

Christopher Love's plot (referred to above) in 1651, spent six months in jail and was then released. He was one of the ministers who suffered the notorious Great Ejection of 1662.

The church which he pastored was destroyed by the fire of 1666. After the Ejection Watson preached wherever it was possible. Those who loved his preaching would gather in barns, kitchens, in back rooms and in the woods to hear the word of life. In 1675 he and Stephen Charnock licensed Crosby Hall for services. In 1686 Watson and his wife Abigail retired to Barnston in Essex where her father was minister. The church building, designed in the old 'meeting-house' style, still exists and

The most readable of the Puritans. For those not acquainted with Puritan authors Watson's '*Body of Divinity*' is the best place to begin. This is a profoundly life-changing book. In a clear illustrative style Watson explains the foremost doctrinal and experimental truths of the Christian faith. Originally Watson's exposition of the Shorter Catechism was in one volume. '*The Ten Commandments*' and '*The Lord's Prayer*' are now published in separate volumes by the Banner of Truth.

it was here that Watson was buried when he died while in prayer later that year.

Watson is highly esteemed as the most readable of the Puritans. He wrote in an original, concise, pithy, pungent, racy, rich and illustrative style. Out of the heart proceeds character. It is in Watson's writings that we detect a minister of superb quality.

The most popular writings by Watson are his *A Body of Divinity, The Lord's Prayer* and *The Ten Commandments.* These books are based on the *Westminster Shorter Catechism.* Also much appreciated is Watson's *All Things for Good* (sometimes called *A Divine Cordial*) and *The Doctrine of Repentance.*[8]

John Owen (1616-1683)

John Owen is deservedly known as 'the Prince of the Puritans'. His *Works* are first choice for those who prize sound divinity. Today his writings are available in twenty-five volumes and together they form the best source of theology in the English language. Owen is also called 'the King David of the Puritans'. We can ascribe this to his overall reliability. He wrote books in response to the challenges and pressures of his times. But in all his writings there is power and cohesion of thought, and always total faithfulness to the authority of Scripture. Many examples can be cited in which Owen is unrivalled for balance and penetration of thought. One example is his great work on *The Person and Work of the Holy Spirit* (*Works*, vol. 3); others are *The Glory of Christ* (vol. 1) and *The Mortification of Sin* (vol. 6). His writing on *Liberty of Conscience* (vol. 13) is as relevant now as it was in his time.

Of Welsh noble background, Owen was so brilliant in intellect that he was sent to Oxford University at the age of twelve. There he studied for ten years. He enjoyed hurling the javelin and competed in the long jump. He also played the flute. His nature as an intense scholar was such that sometimes he only allowed himself four hours' sleep a night. That kind of daily programme does not make for Olympic champions!

While on a visit to London, Owen and some of his friends went to hear the famous preacher Edmund Calamy. They

John Owen

(1616–1683)

were disappointed when Calamy did not arrive. He was replaced by a country preacher. The Holy Spirit used the visitor to bring Owen to personal assurance of salvation.

Owen's first pastorate was at Fordham, a village in Essex. At that time he married Mary Rooke. His family life was immensely sorrowful in a way we could scarcely understand in our day of modern medical science. Of eleven children only one, a girl, survived into adulthood. Her marriage did not work out and she returned to her parents and shortly afterwards died of consumption.

In an amazingly active life, lived through a crucial and decisive period in the political and religious history of England, Owen wrote treatise after treatise to answer the needs of those times. In the process he has given posterity the best resource of reliable theology in the English language.

This portrait is reproduced by courtesy of the Bristol Baptist College.

In 1646 Owen was called to a London congregation where 2,000 attended each Lord's Day. In June 1648 General Fairfax besieged Colchester and Owen was invited to preach to the soldiers. He became friends with many of the officers, including Oliver Cromwell's son-in-law Henry Ireton. Owen's gifts were soon recognized and he was invited to minister before Parliament, where he became the favourite preacher and was appointed chaplain to Oliver Cromwell.

In 1652 he was installed as vice-chancellor of Oxford University. This position involved a wide range of administrative responsibilities. During his six years of tenure he made theology, preaching, catechism and prayer central. The discipline at Oxford was poor and Owen was effective in his work, being tolerant but firm. There was an incident when a student uttered obscenities in a debate. He was warned but continued. Finally Owen himself thrust the student physically from the room!

In 1658 Owen took part in a meeting of ministers from Congregational churches. This conference took place at the Savoy Palace in London. He was appointed with Dr Thomas Goodwin, Philip Nye, William Bridge, William Greenhill and Joseph Caryl (all of whom had been members of the Westminster Assembly) to prepare a confession of faith based on *The Westminster Confession*. This became known as *The Savoy Declaration.*

In 1676 Owen lost his excellent wife by death. Eighteen months later he remarried. His second wife was a woman of wealth. By this time his health was failing and he was able to enjoy the luxury of a carriage for travel.

Owen's writings reveal an analytical, formative and majestic mind. Foundational to all his works is a profound grasp of the doctrines of grace. However John Owen's style is not easy for contemporary readers. A tremendous service has been rendered by R. J. K. Law, who has abridged and modernized some of Owen's best writings: *The Holy Spirit, Communion with God, Apostasy from the Gospel* and *The Glory of Christ.*[9]

Richard Baxter (1615-1691)

Unlike many Puritan leaders who enjoyed the advantage of education in the prestigious universities of Cambridge or Oxford, Baxter had to find his own way educationally. By

Richard Baxter

(1615–1691)

dint of self-discipline he acquired learning which put him on a par with the best Puritan writers.

He was ordained in the Church of England and called to minister in Kidderminster. When he arrived the place was a spiritual desert. He set about his work of visiting and evangelism with incredible zeal. This was used to bring about a marvellous change in the town and necessitated a greatly enlarged auditorium. The Puritans did not use the word 'revival'. Perhaps this work of God's Spirit might be better termed 'a visitation of the Spirit'. There was something about what happened in

Richard Baxter was an energetic pastor and evangelist and a prolific author. His ministry was used to transform the town of Kidderminster. Like Bunyan he was self-taught and lacked the advantages of a university education. Among his best-selling books was 'A Call to the Unconverted' which today is available in modernized form with the title, 'An Invitation to Live'.

Kidderminster which has stimulated and fired the imagination and the fervency of believers ever since.

Baxter married in 1662. His wife, Margaret, was a woman of outstanding spiritual and natural talent and after her death Baxter wrote her biography. Dr Packer eulogizes this biography and suggests that it helps to destroy the caricature that the Puritans were not human. Baxter, more than most, experienced persecution and was subject to imprisonment after the Great Ejection.

During the Civil War Baxter became chaplain to a regiment with Cromwell's forces. For about twenty-five years following the Great Ejection of 1662 Baxter was a leading spokesman for the nonconformists. He was essentially comprehensive in his approach, seeking to keep the various streams together as much as possible. But as a leader in the wider field he was as poor as he was successful on the pastoral side. In May 1685 Baxter was charged before the Lord Chief Justice Jeffreys, on account of his criticisms of the Church of England. Jeffreys, notorious for his hatred of all Puritanism, raved against Baxter and called him 'an old rogue who poisoned the world with his Kidderminster doctrine ... a conceited, stubborn, fanatical dog!' Jeffrey's also expressed his desire that Baxter should be hanged! Had it not been for the influence brought to bear by more reasonable men of power, Baxter might have been whipped through the streets.

During the time when he was silenced in his preaching ministry, he concentrated on writing. His *Christian Directory* is unique inasmuch as it covers every aspect of Christian life from a practical point of view. It is the great 'How to...' book of the Puritans. How does the Christian relate to God, to himself, his family, his church, his work and his nation? With a standard-size page this would come to about 2,000 pages! It is all practical and helpful and provides a guide for us today, as we too need to cover all these practical basic subjects such as marriage and the family, while at the same time grappling with a different set of social problems. The biblical principles are the same but the application needs to be contemporary.

Richard Baxter's evangelistic book *A Call to the Unconverted* was a best seller. Its usefulness continues today.[10] His exposition of Ezekiel 33:11 is extraordinarily perceptive and gripping, typically Puritan. Another outright winner is

Baxter's *The Reformed Pastor*. *The Saints' Everlasting Rest* was also a famous best seller. Baxter's reputation as a Christian writer is based on his devotional and pastoral expositions rather than his works on theological themes.

In his theology, Baxter was individualistic and eccentric and disinclined to submit to others. His errors are not easily detected. In reading the books recommended above we need to learn how to benefit from writers while at the same time avoiding their errors. Packer, who is an expert on the Puritans, and very especially so on Baxter, says of him, 'Baxter was a great and saintly man; as pastor, evangelist, and devotional writer, no praise for him can be too high; but as a theologian he was, though brilliant, something of a disaster. He was Neonomian and Amyraldian.' This was the cause of doctrinal confusion in the next generation. The ramifications of that are beyond our scope at this point but from Baxter's example we are reminded that great care is required in theological formulation. This is precisely why John Owen is so highly valued.

Baxter was not only concerned for evangelism at home. He was just as zealous for missionary work and was a moving power in the establishment of the Society for the Propagation of the Gospel. John Eliot, famous as 'the apostle to the American Indians', found in Baxter a sterling supporter. In his last illness, Baxter read the *Life of Eliot* and wrote to the author, Increase Mather, 'I thought I had been near dying at twelve o'clock in bed; but your book revived me. I knew much of Mr Eliot's opinions, by many letters which I had from him. There was no man on earth I honoured above him. It is his evangelical work that is the apostolic succession for which I plead.'

John Bunyan (1628-1688)

In spiritual experience, in doctrine, in preaching style, and in life, John Bunyan is *the* perfect exemplar of the Puritans.[11]

Born at Elstow, near Bedford, of very poor but respectable parents, Bunyan received a very limited education. At sixteen he lost his mother and a month after that his sister died. Within a month his father remarried. Bunyan became wild and wilful. We know little of his army experience but at the age of sixteen he was recruited into the army by the

John Bunyan

Parliamentary forces for a period of between two and three years.

John Bunyan's testimony of conversion is described in his book *Grace Abounding to the Chief of Sinners.* For instance, having heard a sermon on the importance of the Lord's Day, he went home burdened in spirit. However, he later sallied out to join in a game of 'cat'. As he was in process of striking the stick he seemed to hear a voice from heaven: 'Will you leave your sins and go to heaven, or have your sins and go to hell?' He left the game at once and said he saw the Lord Jesus looking down on him. Yet, for all that, he returned to his habit of playing on the Sabbath and continued unconverted.

John Bunyan (1628–1688)

Bunyan was the most imaginative, eloquent and compelling preacher of his time. The unction that characterized his preaching flows also through his writings. The most famous of these is 'The Pilgrim's Progress', which is second only to the Bible for translation into other languages. Bunyan's complete works have been published in three large handsome volumes by the Banner of Truth. Shut up in a damp prison for twelve years, Bunyan was uncompromising and immovable in his testimony and his love for our Lord Jesus Christ.

Later, overhearing some women speaking about the new birth, he was convicted once more. These same women introduced him to their pastor in Bedford, an excellent man named John Gifford. He was instrumental in leading Bunyan to repentance and faith.

Bunyan's writing style is powerful and his use of English is a delight to every reader. All the phases of prevenient grace appear in *Grace Abounding*: knowledge, illumination (Bunyan never argued with election and predestination or any other Christian doctrine), reformation of life and conviction of sin.

In 1653 Bunyan became a church member and a year later moved to Bedford with his wife and four children, all under six years of age. In 1655 he became a deacon of the church and began to preach. At that time his wife died. In 1660 he was arrested and imprisoned for preaching. Some time before this a godly young woman had agreed to marry him. Although his second wife cared for his children Bunyan was much needed at home. It was agonizing but he refused to compromise his conscience and preferred imprisonment rather than attending the Church of England or quitting his preaching. Twelve years of confinement in prison ensued, from the age of thirty-two to that of forty-four. He especially loved his blind daughter who would come to the prison to work with him to tag shoelaces and in this way help to feed the family.

In prison, where he wrote many fine works, his library consisted of his Bible, a concordance and Foxe's *Book of Martyrs.* In 1674 he was arrested again for preaching the gospel and at that time he began his best-known work, *The Pilgrim's Progress,* a masterpiece and all-time best seller, second only to the Bible. After the Scriptures it is usually the next book to be translated into other languages. Eventually, through the influence and intervention of John Owen, Bunyan was released and saved from a further long term in prison.

As with John Rogers of Dedham, an extraordinary unction attended the preaching of John Bunyan who, taken overall, was the most imaginative, eloquent and compelling preacher of his time. His use of allegory was unique. John Owen said that he would gladly trade all his learning if he could only preach like Bunyan. When he visited London his preaching drew thousands rather than hundreds.

The sheer gripping power of Bunyan's preaching of the gospel is illustrated in his sermons, *The Life and Death of Mr Badman*, *The Jerusalem Sinner Saved* and *Come and Welcome to Jesus Christ*. The latter is on John 6:37 and combines the election of the Father with powerful persuasions to sinners to come to Christ for salvation on the basis that if they come they must know that Christ will never cast them out. His theology was robust and his written works enjoyed popularity equal to that of any of his peers. In *The Jerusalem Sinner Saved* Bunyan enacts the various objections made by the sinners of Jerusalem, disarms those objections and persuades to faith in Christ stressing throughout: '"*Every one of you*! Repent and be baptized *every one of you*!" Objector: "But I was one of them that cried out, 'Crucify him! Crucify him!' and desired that Barabbas, the murderer, might live, rather than him. What will become of me, think you?" Peter: "I am to preach repentance and remission of sins to *every one of you*!"'

I remember hearing a certain Mr Ford who had a fine deep voice and, oddly enough, looked like John Bunyan. He made a special study of Bunyan and memorized sections of his sermons. In a lecture at the Evangelical Library in London he acted out Bunyan's preaching. He included the sermon *The Barren Fig Tree, being the Doom and Downfall of the Fruitless Professor,* in which Bunyan depicts the deathbed of the fruitless professor and the cutting down of the barren fig-tree. I do not think I have ever in my life heard anything as awesome as that.

John Flavel (1627-1691)

Flavel was born of godly parents who died together of the plague in a London prison, where they had been committed for their faith, in 1665. John was educated at Oxford, after which he became a curate at Deptford. He was deprived of his living in 1662 by the Act of Uniformity and subsequently, under much persecution, laboured as a nonconformist pastor in Dartmouth. He enjoyed exceptional unction in prayer and on one occasion wrestled with agonized pleading in public prayer for those going into a sea battle from Dartmouth. The Lord answered his prayer in that there was not one casualty among those who engaged in the battle. His labours

John Flavel

(1627–1691)

were crowned with many conversions, some of which were extraordinary.

It is for his writing that he is now remembered. His works were published in six volumes in 1820 and reissued in 1968.[12] In typical Puritan style, all his written work was first produced in sermon form. Flavel's writings are of outstanding quality. Most compelling is his exposition of Revelation 3:20: 'Behold, I stand at the door and knock; if any man hear my voice, and open the door, I will come in to him, and will sup with him, and he with me.' Eleven superb expositions of Proverbs 4:23, 'Keep thy heart with all diligence, for out of it are the issues of life', total about 260 pages. Best known of all Flavel's writings is *The Mystery of Providence.*[13] Of prime place among his works is *The Fountain of Life*, expositions on the life and sayings of Christ.

The finest memorial to Flavel is the valuable and handsome six-volume set of his complete works published by the Banner of Truth. His series on Revelation 3:20, 'Behold I stand at the door and knock,' is masterly and typical of his warm evangelistic style. Flavel's work *The Mystery of Providence* has stirred, edified and comforted readers over many years and continues to be enjoyed.

Hanserd Knollys (1599-1691)

Like John Bunyan, Hanserd Knollys was a Puritan. Also like Bunyan he was a Baptist. Through Knollys Baptists today can trace their own historical connections to the vast and rich legacy of the Puritan testimony and the inheritance of Puritan literature.

Hanserd Knollys

(1599-1691)

Knollys was blessed with good health and energy throughout his exceedingly active life. His name is the first signature of thirty-seven to record agreement and unity in the publication of the second London Baptist Confession of Faith (now published in modern English as A Faith to Confess).

Knollys died at the advanced age of ninety-three. His life spans the seventeenth century. He was one of seven who put their signature to *The First London Baptist Confession of Faith* in 1646 and his name heads a list of thirty-seven to record agreement and unity in the publication of *The Second London Baptist Confession of Faith* in 1689. Indeed, although advanced in age, Knollys was a prime mover in organizing a National Assembly of Calvinistic Baptists on the occasion of the accession to the throne of William III and the passing of the Toleration Act in 1689. *The 1689 Confession* was actually formulated in 1677 but persecution prevented it from being published at that time. This confession follows *The Westminster Confession* in all chapters except four which concern believers' baptism, the nature of the church and church government.

Hanserd Knollys was one of the few Baptists in the line of the Puritans who received a university education. He studied at St Catherine's College, Cambridge. He testified, 'I prayed daily, heard all the godly ministers I could, read and searched the holy Scriptures, read good books, and got acquainted with gracious Christians then called Puritans.' Knollys was ordained and appointed minister of a parish in Lincolnshire. He resigned in 1631 because of his Puritan convictions. He could not in good conscience follow the rituals required and could not agree to 'admitting wicked persons to the Lord's Supper'.

Benjamin Brook devotes eleven pages to Knollys in his three-volume work *The Lives of the Puritans*. Brook writes, 'About the year 1636 Knollys left the Church entirely. He renounced his Episcopal ordination, and joined himself to the Puritans. This exposed him to numerous difficulties and hardships. He was driven out of Lincolnshire, and at length out of the kingdom, for his nonconformity.' When he arrived in America he had no money but his wife had, unknown to him, saved five pounds. In 1641 he returned to England in poverty but he opened a school which after a year was attended by 156 scholars. It was at this time that he became associated with the Calvinistic Baptists.

Knollys was a courageous preacher. On one of his preaching tours in Suffolk he was stoned. During the 1640s Knollys was a leading apologist in defending the Reformed position (as held by John Calvin and Martin Bucer) against the fanatical claims of the Seekers. Their claims were similar to those of extreme charismatics today. The Seekers claimed that because of apostasy God had withdrawn signs, wonders and miracles, raising of the dead and prophecies. Knollys' very able defence of the orthodox position that the apostolic age and apostolic gifts (Heb. 2:4; 2 Cor. 12:12) were unique was set out in his book *The Shining of a Flaming Fire in Zion*.

Knollys maintained that James 5:14 is our guide in the case of special need and he himself possessed an unusual faith and a remarkable gift of prayer, which are seen in many remarkable petitions, especially during the time of the Great Plague. Towards the end of Knollys' life the famous leader Benjamin Keach was taken ill to the point of death. Knollys visited him and implored the Lord to spare him in the same way that he had spared King Hezekiah. Keach recovered and lived another fifteen years.

During the unsettled time of 1660 Knollys was imprisoned for eighteen weeks in Newgate Prison. Later, when he was in Holland, his property was confiscated but he once more opened a school in order to recover financially. He was imprisoned again in 1670. He possessed exceptional bodily stamina. In prison he would preach every day. When not in prison he preached three or four times every Lord's Day and many times during the week. He was noted for the cheerfulness and courage with which he bore persecutions and sufferings. Right to the end of his life he was actively encouraging his flock and advancing the wider cause of Christ.

Henry Jessey (1601-1663)

In his *History of the Puritans* Daniel Neal describes Mr Henry Jessey as 'an eminent divine among the Puritans'.

Henry Jessey was born in 1601 near Cleveland, in Yorkshire, where his father was minister. At seventeen years of age he was sent to St John's College, Cambridge. When his father died in 1623 he was left with only three pence a day to live on. While at university he showed mastery in the biblical languages and later, with friends, set himself to translate the whole Bible. This enterprise, though almost completed, did not result in publication. It was said of Jessey that the original languages of the Old and New Testament were as familiar to him as his mother tongue. After leaving Cambridge he worked as a chaplain in an aristocratic home. He was ordained in 1627. In 1633 he accepted the living of Aughton in Yorkshire, but soon he was in trouble. His Puritan convictions caused him to take down a crucifix and he refused to follow the prescribed order of service. He was dismissed and thereafter received into the home of Sir Matthew Bointon in Yorkshire from where he preached frequently in two parishes.

In 1635 Jessey was invited to be pastor of the congregation formed in 1616 by Henry Jacob. He continued in this position until his death. A number in the congregation had accepted believers' baptism and this stirred Jessey to study the subject. Neal says, 'After great deliberation, many prayers and frequent conferences with pious and learned

Henry Jessey

(1601-1663).

It was said of Jessey that the original languages of the Old and New Testament were as familiar to him as his mother tongue. He showed deep concern for the Jews and collected a large sum of money to relieve the needs of Jews who were suffering in Jerusalem.

friends, he altered his sentiments, first concerning the mode, and then the subjects, of baptism. But he maintained the same temper of friendship and charity towards other Christians, not only as to conversation, but church-communion. When he visited churches in the north and west of England, he laboured to promote the spirit of love and union among them and was a principal person in setting up and maintaining, for some time, a meeting of some eminent men of each denomination in London.'

In June 1645 he was baptized by Hanserd Knollys. In London, in addition to his own pastorate, he ministered regularly at St George's Church, Southwark, and at other places during the week.

He deliberately chose to be single so that he could devote his life to serving others. Perhaps his experience of extreme poverty as a student was partly responsible for his sympathy for, and amazing generosity to, the poor. Thirty poor families received their support from him and so remarkable was his passion to help the needy that he collected

£300 (a large sum in those days) for Jews in desperate need in Jerusalem. With this gift he sent letters of concern. Later he wrote a treatise proving that Jesus is the true Messiah. This was prepared in Hebrew for distribution among Jews wherever they might be found.

Upon the Restoration he was ejected from his position at St George's. He was silenced in his ministry and committed to prison. About six months later he died full of peace and joy. Neal reports that several thousand, of many different persuasions, attended his funeral.

John Howe (1630-1705)

John Howe was a graduate of Cambridge and Oxford, At the age of twenty-six he became a domestic chaplain to Oliver Cromwell. In 1662 he was ejected from Torrington in Devon and subsequently became one of the foremost leaders of nonconformity.

For several years before receiving a call in 1671 to Antrim in Ireland, Howe struggled to support his increasing family. The call was to become chaplain to Lord Massarene. Howe was described by a friend as an incomparable preacher and this is illustrated by an incident on the journey to Ireland. Bad weather prevented the ship from sailing and in the meantime Howe was invited to preach in the town. A large crowd gathered. Such was the impact made that the next week when the ship was still delayed a huge crowd gathered and although Howe was ill he sought the Lord's enabling and preached again with great freedom. He testified that never in his experience had he seen a congregation so moved, or receiving the Word with such pleasure. Permission to preach every Lord's Day in the parish church at Antrim was obtained without Howe having to compromise his principles of nonconformity.

In 1675 he was called to a church in London. Some of his sermons created much interest and after his death his principal works were gathered together for publication.[14]

other
well-known Puritans

The writer of the letter to the Hebrews expressed his dilemma as he described believers in the Old Testament. His problem was whom to omit. There were so many worthy characters who excelled in the exercise of their faith. He mentions the names of just a few and then has to leave it (Heb. 11:32). In the same way, many worthy Puritans have not been described in this book. It will help at this point to place or mention some of the better-known of these men.

William Ames (1576-1633) took refuge in Holland, where he spent most of his ministerial career. His book *The Marrow of Theology* was extraordinarily popular, especially in New England. Some of the better-known New England Puritans were Thomas Hooker, Thomas Shepherd, John Davenport, Increase Mather and Cotton Mather.

Among the Puritans who participated in the Westminster Assembly were William Twisse (chairman), Anthony Burgess, Edmund Calamy, Joseph Caryl, Simeon Ashe, Philip Nye, Obadiah Sedgwick and Stephen Marshall. Daniel Cawdrey and Herbert Palmer were delegated the task of writing on the subject of the Sabbath, on which subject they produced two volumes. There were five representatives from Scotland at the Assembly, among whom were Samuel Rutherford and Alexander Henderson.

William Gurnall is famous on account of his classic, *The Christian in Complete Armour,* William Jenkyn for his commentary on Jude, Thomas Taylor for his on Titus, and Richard Alleine for his book *Heaven Opened.* The northern Puritan Isaac Ambrose was well known especially for his classic, *Looking unto Jesus.* Oliver Heywood, also from northern England, kept diaries which form a valuable source of information about the Puritan way of life.

Matthew Poole is renowned on account of his complete commentary on the Bible. Matthew Henry, equally famous for his *Commentary on the whole Bible,* was the son of the Puritan Philip Henry. John Owen was followed in his last pastorate in London by David Clarkson, whose writings have been republished in three volumes.

Christopher Love, a wonderfully gifted young Welsh preacher, was executed in 1651 by beheading, at the age of thirty-three. He was charged with being involved in raising money to restore the monarchy. Arrested at the same time on suspicion of conspiracy were Puritan pastors Thomas Watson, William Jenkyn and Ralph Robinson. They were released. Ralph Robinson's sermons on the glory of Christ have been republished. He once said to an intimate friend that he loved fasting and prayer with all his heart.

Some well-known Puritans died young: for example, James Janeway at thirty-eight and the very able and popular preacher John Preston at thirty-one. In Scotland gifted preaching and writing Puritans James Durham and Hugh Binning died at the ages of thirty-six and twenty-six respectively. Joseph Alleine departed to be with Christ when he was only thirty-four. He is famous on account of the popularity of his book, *An Alarm to the Unconverted,* hundreds of editions of which have been published.

The demise of the Puritan movement

As we saw in 'the Story of the Puritans', an act was passed in 1662 which demanded conformity to the Church of England. Clergymen who had not been episcopally ordained were to be re-ordained. Assent was required to every part of *The Book of Common Prayer.* Every minister was required to take the oath of canonical obedience and to renounce 'The Solemn League and Covenant', which was a pledge for reformation usually printed alongside the text of *The Westminster Confession of Faith* and *The Westminster Catechisms.* The new Act of Uniformity was aimed to ensure that reformation be renounced.

Of course the consciences of the Puritans could not submit to these requirements. About 2,000 — the great majority of them ministers, but also a number of men who held positions of authority, such as headmasters and teachers in schools — were forced out of their occupations. To avoid destitution they had to resort to any kind of work they could find. It was a terrible time.

It was the end of Puritanism as such. A new era known as 'Dissent' began. By the end of the seventeenth century the demise of Puritanism was virtually complete. Of the well-known Puritans who lived to see the eighteenth century were John Howe (died 1705), whose life we have just reviewed, and Thomas Doolittle, who died in 1707. Matthew Henry, famous for his commentary on the whole Bible, was the son of Philip Henry (1631-1696), one of the Puritans ejected in 1662. Matthew, who for a while studied under Thomas Doolittle in Islington, London, was born in 1662 and died in 1714.[15]

The sufferings caused by the Great Ejection of 1662 and the severe and relentless persecution that ensued until 1688 broke up the unity of the evangelicals and severely restricted the benefits of a well-trained ministry. Nonconformists were barred from the universities and this had an adverse effect on the standards of the ministry. The cogent spiritual unity which had characterized the Puritans went into steep decline after 1662. The Calvinism of the Puritans had been well balanced and evangelistic. After the 1662 Ejection,

Arminianism began to predominate in the churches and in due course that gave way to Unitarianism. Those faithful pastors who were ejected continued to write but when that generation of great leaders passed away there were few to take their place.

The Church of England has never recovered from the Ejection of 1662. From time to time there have been exceptional leaders like Bishop J. C. Ryle (1816-1900). Ryle followed the emphases of the Puritans and wrote like a Puritan. His well-known book with the title *Holiness* provides expository material on the Puritan doctrine of sanctification.

The brightest son born to Puritanism in the nineteenth century was C. H. Spurgeon and in the twentieth Dr Martyn Lloyd-Jones. Spurgeon was steeped in, and fashioned by, the writings and principles of the Puritans, and can only be understood in that light.[16] Puritanism went into steep decline and was almost extinct for the first half of the twentieth century. Spurgeon anticipated this decline when he declared, 'Out of the present contempt into which Puritanism has fallen many brave hearts and true will fetch it, by the help of God, ere many years have passed. Those who have daubed up the windows will yet be surprised to see Heaven's light breaking forth from it to their own confusion.'[17]

Interest in the Puritans and their literature began to spread in the late 1950s and has increased since then. Without a theological renewal this would not have been possible.[18] Dr Martyn Lloyd-Jones' interest in the Puritans was first awakened in 1925 when he read a biography of Richard Baxter. Dr Lloyd-Jones propagated interest in the Puritans on a wide scale. His papers delivered at the Puritan Conference, nineteen in all, have been printed in a volume with the title *The Puritans.*[19]

Dr James I. Packer has contributed much to encourage interest in the Puritans. As a first-year student at Oxford in 1944 Jim Packer was appointed a junior librarian to assess and house a Puritan library that had been donated to OICCU (Oxford Inter-Collegiate Christian Union). It was then he discovered the twenty-four-volume set of John Owen. The pages were uncut. The contents were summarized on the spines. In order to read about mortification of sin Packer first cut his way into volume 6. That was his rediscovery of the Puritans. Later he wrote a doctoral thesis on Richard Baxter. In due course Packer's contribution towards a revival of interest in the Puritans was immense. His work on the Puritans is gathered together in his book *Among God's Giants*.[20]

Puritanism brings together in beautiful proportion the precious truths of Scripture, a proportion of doctrine, experience and practice which exalts Jesus Christ who is the Truth (John 14:6). It is the will of the Holy Spirit to glorify Christ and for this reason we can be sure that the promises will be fulfilled, as Isaiah declares:

> The least of you will become a thousand,
> the smallest a mighty nation.
> I am the LORD;
> in its time I will do this swiftly
>
> (Isa. 60:22).

And Habakkuk:

> For the earth will be filled with the knowledge of the glory of the LORD,
> As the waters cover the sea
>
> (Hab. 2:14).

Part III

Help from the Puritans

1. The Westminster Confession and justification

The Westminster Confession of Faith forms the doctrinal basis of many Presbyterian denominations, and its equivalents *The 1689 London Baptist Confession* and *The Savoy Declaration* have been adopted by Reformed Baptist and Congregational churches respectively.

Beside serving as a doctrinal basis for local churches, the Puritan Confessions of Faith serve to give a sense of historical continuity. A Confession of Faith provides a useful teaching aid to ensure that the whole counsel of God's Word is preached. The Puritan Confessions can be useful to express the unity of Reformed churches. This was in fact the original principal purpose of *The 1689 London Baptist Confession.* A confession is also a means by which doctrinal integrity can be maintained. It was the grief of Charles Haddon Spurgeon during the Downgrade Controversy of 1887-1892 that the Baptist Union would have nothing to do with defining doctrine. It is impossible to defend the truth without being definitive. We shall see how important clarity and definition are as we take up the subject of justification by faith, which is God's way of salvation.

We can gain help from many chapters in the Puritan Confessions but because of its cardinal place we will begin by examining justification and observing the relevance of the doctrine for today.

Justification by faith alone

From their writings we can see that the Reformers and Puritans regarded justification as *articulus stantis vel cadentis ecclesiae* — the point on which depends the standing or falling of the church. Enshrined in the heart of Protestant Confessions of Faith, especially the three mentioned above, is the doctrine of justification by faith alone. It would be difficult to find any Puritan who was as eloquent on justification as Luther, but in principle they followed him. Thomas Watson asserted that 'Justification is the very hinge and pillar of Christianity,'[1] and John Owen found time to expound and defend the doctrine in a 400-page treatise.[2]

Luther declared, 'This is the chief article from which all other doctrines have flowed,' and argued, 'It alone begets, nourishes, builds, preserves, and defends the Church of God: and without it the Church cannot exist for one hour.' He contended that 'When the article of justification has fallen, everything has fallen.'[3] The reason for this is that if there is confusion about justification by faith in Christ alone then, instead of looking to Christ alone, enquirers are left to seek salvation in sources which cannot save. In other words, to be obscure at this point is to open the door to darkness and confusion. Justification by faith alone concerns the very character and attributes of God because justification shows that God requires perfect holiness. Justification directly concerns all the work of Christ, since the righteousness which is imputed to the believer consists of the active and passive obedience of our Redeemer.

A modern English version of *The Westminster Confession* defines justification as follows:

> God freely justifies the persons whom he effectually calls. He does this, not by infusing righteousness into them but by pardoning their sins and by accounting them, and accepting them as righteous. This he does for Christ's sake alone and not for

> anything wrought in them or done by them. The righteousness which is imputed to them, that is, reckoned to their account, is neither their faith nor the act of believing nor any obedience to the gospel which they have rendered, but Christ's obedience alone. Christ's one obedience is twofold — his active obedience rendered to the entire divine law, and his passive obedience rendered in his death.

The Confession goes on to assert, 'The faith which receives and rests on Christ and his righteousness is the sole means of justification. Yet it is never alone in the person justified, but is invariably accompanied by all other saving graces.' The Puritans maintained firmly the necessity of clarity and the primacy of forensic justification, yet they constantly maintained the juxtaposition of justification and sanctification.

In Romans chapter 6 Paul deals with the objection made to justification, namely, that if a person is forgiven all his sins, past, present and future, and is justified once and for all, will that not make him careless? Will he not say, 'Let us sin that grace may abound'? The answer Paul provides is that union with Christ simultaneously brings both justification and sanctification. The moment a person is joined to Christ by faith he receives righteousness which is the ground of his justification. At the same time the Holy Spirit takes up residence within him to commence the work of holiness. Any person united to Christ will have both justification, which is forensic, external and perfect, and sanctification, which is experimental, internal and imperfect. Hence James insists that any justified person must produce good works as a proof of the reality of his faith.

The clearest definition of justification is found in *The Westminster Larger Catechism*:

> *Question 70:* What is justification?
>
> *Answer*: Justification is an act of God's free grace to sinners, in which he pardons all their sins and accepts them as righteous in his sight; not for anything wrought in them, or done by them, but only for the perfect obedience and full satisfaction of Christ, imputed to them by God, and received by faith alone.

Having summarized the Puritan teaching, I will briefly explain the doctrine by comparing justification and sanctification, both of which are brought into existence simultaneously as the believer is united to Christ by faith. However, it is vital that we observe the distinction between positional and progressive sanctification. Calling into union with Christ, regeneration, justification and adoption are acts of God effected once for all. These acts cannot be repeated. You cannot be fifty per cent justified or fifty per cent adopted. Positional sanctification is the fact of being set apart in Christ. 'Sanctify' means 'to set apart'. There are many references, about twenty in the Old Testament and eighty in the New, to 'saints'. These are references to a definitive action, a single event that has taken place. For instance, the believers at Corinth are addressed as 'those who are sanctified in Christ Jesus, called to be saints' (1 Cor. 1:2, NKJV). In the following comparison it is progressive sanctification that is in view. Examples of texts which call for progressive sanctification are: 'Let us purify ourselves from everything that contaminates body and spirit, perfecting holiness out of reverence for God' (2 Cor. 7:1); and Paul's prayer: 'May God himself, the God of peace, sanctify you through and through. May your whole spirit, soul and body be kept blameless at the coming of our Lord Jesus Christ' (1 Thess. 5:23).

Justification	**Sanctification**
is legal (forensic)	is experimental
is external (like a garment)	is internal
is perfect	is never perfect in this life
is of the Father who declares the believer to be just	is of the Holy Spirit who works in the believer to make him holy
allows of no increase; the believer is justified absolutely and once for all	is progressive
cannot implant anything	cannot impute anything

The Puritans set us an example in upholding the following four principles necessary for a healthy doctrine of justification.

1. Justification must be kept in the context of Scripture as a whole

John Owen is brilliant in his treatment of Romans 5:12-21, as he compares Adam with Christ, and the condemnation of the fallen race in Adam with the justification of the redeemed race in Christ.[4] Owen keeps the whole history of redemption in view and he expounds every crucial text germane to justification. A summary of what takes up 400 pages follows.

Abraham was justified by faith: 'Abram believed the LORD, and he credited it to him as righteousness' (Gen. 15:6). Abraham is a prototype for all who believe, which is why he is called 'the father of all who believe' (Rom. 4:11). Note that righteousness is not infused into Abraham, but rather is put to his credit. Abraham as the prototype of justification is taken up by Paul (Rom. 4:3; Gal 3:6) and by James (2:23). This does not mean that Abraham was the first to be saved by faith. Noah is described as 'an heir of the righteousness that comes by faith' (Heb. 11:7) and 'By faith [Abel] was commended as a righteous man' (Heb. 11:4). But for the sake of clarity Abraham is the primary model referred to in the New Testament.

The letter to the Romans introduces God's salvation as the good news which is the revelation from heaven of God's righteousness which saves. It is a righteousness which he puts to the account of everyone who believes (Rom. 1:16-17). This righteousness was procured by the propitiation of Christ's death (Rom. 3:25). Paul demonstrates that this way of justifying sinners was not new. That is the way Abraham and David were justified (Rom. 4:1-8). The words used to describe justification are words used in a law court.

Paul's explanation of justification is presented in three epistles. Justification is unfolded systematically in Romans, defended in Galatians and extolled in Philippians (Phil. 3:4-11). Paul declares that if anyone could have obtained righteousness by the way of human merit he could have done so, because with regard to observing the law he was 'legalistically faultless', but he came to regard all his self-righteousness as mere rubbish.

To the question put by Job, 'How can a man be just before God?' (Job 9:2), there are only two possible answers. The first is self-justification on account of good works of one kind or another. The second is God's justification on account of the righteousness that he has provided in his Son. Universally mankind by nature seeks the way of self-justification. This reality is stressed in the New Testament and the apostles clearly taught that human merit is doomed as a basis of justification. Paul tried the way of human merit and he said that Israel went about to seek their own righteousness because they were ignorant of God's righteousness (Rom. 10:3).[5]

2. Justification depends on fidelity to the biblical terms

Justification is essentially forensic. As Thomas Watson says in his quaint way, 'It is *verbum forense'*, a word borrowed from the law courts.[6] Justification concerns a person's legal standing, not his internal condition. When we are uncertain about the ownership of our property we visit our legal representatives or lawyers, not the medical clinic.

The meaning and use of the Greek verb *dikaioo*, to justify, and its derivatives are essentially legal in character. John Owen, as no other writer, examines in detail both the Hebrew and Greek words used in setting out this doctrine. He demonstrates that these terms denote a legal status employed to mean acquittal, or pronouncing someone righteous.[7]

But the true and genuine signification of these words is to be determined from those in the original languages of the Scripture which are expounded by them. In the Hebrew it is צָדַק. This the LXX. render by *Δίκαιον ἀποφαίνω*, Job xxvii. 5; *Δίκαιος ἀναφαίνομαι*, chap. xiii. 18; *Δίκαιον κρίνω*, Prov. xvii. 15;—to show or declare one righteous; to appear righteous; to judge any one righteous. And the sense may be taken from any one of them, as Job xiii. 18, הִנֵּה־נָא עָרַכְתִּי מִשְׁפָּט יָדַעְתִּי כִּי־אֲנִי אֶצְדָּק,—"Behold, now I have ordered my cause; I know that I shall be justified." The ordering of his cause (his judgment), his cause to be judged on, is his preparation for a sentence, either of absolution or condemnation: and hereon his confidence was, that he should be justified; that is, *absolved, acquitted, pronounced righteous.* And the sense is no less pregnant in the other places. Commonly, they render it by *δικαιόω*· whereof I shall speak afterward.

For instance, we read in Luke 7:29, 'When all the people heard [John the Baptist], even the tax collectors justified God, having been baptized by him' (Luke 7:29). This does not mean that the tax collectors somehow changed God's nature, but rather that they declared that God was righteous. A striking example of sinners being declared righteous on account of another is 2 Corinthians 5:21: 'God made him who had no sin to be sin for us, so that in him we might become the righteousness of God.' The nature of the transaction is complete and perfect. Justification admits of no degrees. I am not partially justified, or half-justified; I am justified! I am 'in Christ' and on that basis his righteousness is imputed to me. Similarly there is the example of a man being accused by Satan on account of his guilt. But God justifies that man because his Son bore the penalty which is his due (Rom. 8:33). Justification is the act of God the Father. If he justifies the sinner who can refute that?

A further outstanding example is the illustration of our Lord when he describes the Pharisee and the tax collector who went up to the temple to pray. The Pharisee congratulated himself on his superiority but the tax collector prayed, literally, 'God be propitiated to me a sinner.' Jesus assures us that the tax collector went home justified.

There are two aspects of justification. The first is acquittal, the remission of all sin. The second is the constitution of the sinner as righteous. This meaning is powerfully asserted in Romans 5:19, 'Through the obedience of the one man the many will be made (*katastathesontai* — will be constituted) righteous.'

The picture used in Revelation 3:5, 'They will walk with me, dressed in white,' is a most appropriate portrayal of Christ's righteousness. The remission of sin proceeds from the passive obedience of Christ, his offering up of himself as the propitiation for our sins. Christ's active obedience provides that righteousness which constitutes the believer righteous. It is human righteousness. The incarnation was essential. As man he lived out righteousness for us throughout his life on earth.

William Bridge states the matter clearly. He poses the question, 'Are we justified by the passive righteousness of Christ only?' and continues, 'I answer, we are not justified by the passive obedience of Christ only: there are two essential parts in justification, namely remission of sin, and imputation of righteousness. By Christ's redemption, the guilt is taken away, and by his active obedience the believing person is made completely righteous in the sight of God.'[8]

3. Justification must be related to the Christian life

Paul continues, in his systematic thesis on justification in Romans 5, to outline the blessings of justification. From his description it is clear that the whole Christian life is based on justification. According to Paul in Romans 5:1-11, each of the following aspects of the Christian life springs directly from the foundation of justification:

1. The Christian's relationship with God is peace.
2. The Christian is privileged to enjoy a life of prayer with immediate access to God.
3. The Christian is assured that his sufferings produce perseverance and character.
4. The Christian enjoys the love of the Father, a love of adoption poured into his heart.
5. The Christian is assured that he will persevere. His union with Christ, by which he received justification, is the union which guarantees his perseverance.

All the above are related to assurance and spiritual experience. How do I know I am justified? Thomas Goodwin wrote extensively on the relationship of faith and assurance. True saving faith may lack assurance. Both Thomas Goodwin and John Owen had a struggle to attain a full assurance of faith. This theme is developed separately so I will not digress here other than to commend Goodwin's work, *The Object and Acts of Justifying Faith.*[9]

4. The relationship of justification to sanctification must be maintained

The fact that the church in the early and middle centuries was not clear about forensic justification does not alter the fact that the Scripture places justification in a primary position.[10] Due to Augustine's ignorance of Greek a crippling error was perpetuated. Augustine interpreted the Latin verb *justificare* as 'to *make* righteous'. Justification, as we have seen, means 'to *declare* righteous'. Thus instead of promoting the glorious liberating doctrine of justification, which was so powerfully proclaimed by Martin Luther, the teaching focussed on the inward and the subjective.

As we have seen, justification is the imputation of Christ's righteousness to the believer. If a good work of any kind whatsoever is added as necessary for justification that immediately nullifies the doctrine. As Paul says, 'For if righteousness could be gained through the law, Christ died for nothing' (Gal. 2:21).[11] 'By the deeds of the law no flesh will be justified in his sight' (Rom. 3:20, NKJV).

Justification is made null and void if it is confused with sanctification and understood to mean that the person is actually made righteous, which is, and always has been, the teaching of the Roman Catholic Church. John Owen shows that the Roman Catholic doctrine is based on the idea of two justifications.[12] The first is baptism, defined by Rome as the infusion of grace by which original sin is extinguished and all habits of sin are expelled. The second justification is the righteousness of good works whereby the righteous merit eternal life. This second stage of justification is regarded as an ongoing process throughout the person's life which includes recourse to the 'sacrament of penance' and after death purification by the fires of purgatory. An examination of the new Roman Catholic Catechism of 1994 shows that there is no change whatsoever in this understanding of justification.[13]

John Owen shows how the Roman Catholic teaching supplants justification by faith alone: 'The gratuitous pardon of sin and imputation of Christ's righteousness once and for all is utterly defeated.'[14] The assurance of eternal life is eliminated by dependence on this uncertain process which in the end requires to be completed in the fires of purgatory. The biblical doctrine of justification nurtures assurance so strong that in Romans chapter 8 all opposition is defied: 'Who shall bring a charge against God's elect? It is God who justifies. Who is he who condemns? It is Christ who died, and furthermore is also risen, who is even at the right hand of God, who also makes intercession for us' (Rom. 8:33-34, NKJV).

A modern challenge to justification

In America there is a society known as ECT — *Evangelicals and Catholics Together*. On 20 November 1998 a group of evangelical and Roman Catholic leaders convened a conference in which they presented two documents which they claimed spelled out a basis of co-operation and unity which would include joint evangelism. Father Francis Martin represented the Roman Catholics and Dr James I. Packer represented evangelicals. Dr Robert Godfrey, president of Westminster Seminary West, represented evangelicals with 'serious concerns' about the statements undergirding ECT.

ECT produced a five-point statement which affirms several notable truths about justification yet falls short of the biblical doctrine of justification by faith alone. The Roman Catholic Church has always contended that Christ's righteousness is infused rather than imputed. The decrees of the Council of Trent anathematized all who hold to justification by faith alone:

> *Canon 9.* If anyone says that the sinner is justified by faith alone, meaning that nothing else is required to co-operate in order to obtain the grace of justification, and that it is not in any way necessary that he be prepared and disposed by the action of his own will, let him be anathema.

These canons have never been renounced and Dr Godfrey exposed the fact that the new statement opens the door to infused righteousness and does nothing to renounce the canons of Trent. For those reasons he expressed his utter opposition to the present stance of ECT. He deplored the fact that Dr J. I. Packer, while agreeing with the biblical doctrine of justification by faith alone, is prepared to compromise when it comes to practice.

This movement of ECT, which originated in America, has a worldwide impact. For example, Noel Espinosa, principal of Grace Ministerial Academy in the Philippines, reports, 'Traditional evangelicals and evangelical charismatics have found justification for their inclusivist approach in the document, *Evangelicals and Catholics Together*. No longer are Catholics seen as the objects of gospel mission; they have become fellow-missionaries.'[15]

How much should we care about justification?

John Owen declares that justification by faith alone includes a sincere renunciation of all other ways and means.[16] No greater sacrifice could be made than that of God's Son. That is the heart of the matter. The gift of God's Son was a perfect gift, and his sacrifice a perfect sacrifice. 'When this priest had offered for all time one sacrifice for sins, he sat down at the right hand of God' (Heb. 10:12). In the Father's wisdom he has made him to be our righteousness (justification), holiness (sanctification) and redemption (1 Cor. 1:21).

When we embrace this sacrifice and receive the righteousness of the Son who made the sacrifice, we renounce all other ways of seeking to obtain salvation. Hence Peter insists, 'Salvation is found in no one else, for there is no other name under heaven given to men by which we must be saved' (Acts 4:12). 'The LORD is our righteousness' (Jer. 23:6). The psalmist declares, 'I will proclaim your righteousness, yours alone' (Ps. 71:16). Accompanying this righteousness is a repudiation of all self-righteousness: 'All our righteous acts are like filthy rags' (Isa. 64:6).

After the demise of Puritanism a period of deep spiritual depression followed. But then came the evangelical revival of the eighteenth century, and with it the writing of hymns which extol the truths of imputed righteousness. John Wesley translated von Zinzendorf's great hymn, the following verses of which epitomize our subject:

Jesus, thy blood and righteousness
My beauty are, my glorious dress;
Midst flaming worlds, in these arrayed,
With joy shall I lift up my head.

This spotless robe the same appears
When ruined nature sinks in years;
No age can change its spotless hue,
The robe of Christ is ever new.

Many seek the power of God today in miracles, signs and wonders, but our God constantly reveals his power *in the gospel*, which Paul proclaims to be God's power in the salvation of everyone who believes. He goes on to declare that in the preaching of the gospel the righteousness of God is being revealed — present tense.[17] In the preaching of the gospel of justification by faith alone the church of Christ possesses her greatest asset for changing the whole world.

In the preaching of the gospel of justification by faith alone the church of Christ possesses her greatest asset for changing the whole world.

2.
The Puritans and a stable doctrine of divine sovereignty and human responsibility

The errors of Arminianism have prevailed in Western Christianity over the last hundred years or more. Inevitably these errors have been carried to the mission-fields. The theological renewal since the 1960s has seen a recovery of the Reformed faith. However, in this recovery a small minority have fallen into hyper-Calvinism.[1]

A most important legacy from the Puritans is a stable doctrine of divine sovereignty and human responsibility. The Puritans were well versed in the debate over Arminianism which took place at the Synod of Dort 1618-1619 in the city of Dordrecht in the Netherlands. William Laud (1573-1645) was Archbishop of Canterbury from 1633. He was the arch-promoter of Arminianism. From about 1633 the Puritans were put to the test as far as Arminianism was concerned.

In more recent times a decisive book in the Puritan tradition has been *Evangelism and the Sovereignty of God* by J. I. Packer. This exposition has been widely used to preserve the Reformed movement from hyper-Calvinism.[2] Packer uses the term 'antinomy' to describe two seemingly contradictory concepts which are in fact not contradictory but fully compatible. He uses the analogy of light. As light consists of rays and particles in a way which is inexplicable to human reason, so divine sovereignty and human responsibility exist together in a way which can only be held by faith (Isa. 55:8-9). The human rationality of the hyper-Calvinist insists on explanations and this insistence drives him to unbiblical conclusions. That is intolerable.

A stable view will prevent wrong conclusions and misguided practice. Divine sovereignty in salvation and human responsibility must be held together. Wrong conclusions can easily destabilize the truth of the gospel.

The first set of wrong conclusions concerns the nature of man as a consequence of the Fall. Does man have free will towards God, or is he crippled by his enmity to God and his law? If he is crippled is he still fully responsible for his attitudes and actions?

The second set of wrong conclusions concerns the sovereignty of God. Does not God's sovereignty in salvation lead inevitably to a fatalistic mind-set? The reasoning here is that if God is sovereign then there is nothing that man can do. Also if God is sovereign and alone decides the issue of salvation does that mean his love is limited only to the elect, or does he love all mankind? Does his sovereign purpose to save only some mean that he is insincere in the free offers of the gospel to all sinners indiscriminately?

1. Wrong thinking about free will

The Puritan doctrine of salvation by grace is enshrined in *The Westminster Confession of Faith* and its parallel expression in *The London Baptist 1689 Confession of Faith.* A number of chapters are devoted to salvation: chapter 9 to free will, chapters 10-14 to the redemption God bestows by grace, and chapters 14-17 to the graces man exercises. In this compass we see the necessity of divine intervention to save fallen man. We observe at the same time that the fall into sin does not annul human responsibility.

The Puritan Confessions each devote a chapter to free will. This was a central issue in the Reformation. In his response to Erasmus Martin Luther wrote a book with the title *The Bondage of the Will.* In this Luther asserted that free will was the hinge on which the whole controversy about the source of salvation turned. That is as true today as it was then. J. I. Packer said of Luther's *Bondage of the Will* that it is the classical elucidation of what the Reformation conflict was all about, and B. B. Warfield said of it that it is in a true sense the manifesto of the Reformation. The Arminian idea is that salvation is decided by the free will of man, and not by the sovereign grace of God. In other words, salvation is of man and not of God, whereas the Scripture makes it clear that it is by grace that we are saved and not of ourselves (Eph. 2:8-9).

The chapter in the Confessions devoted to the subject of free will contains five paragraphs. We are reminded that our first parents possessed free will but the possibility existed of their falling. As a consequence of the Fall man plunged into the bondage and slavery of sin which is now the state of his will, a will ruled by the sinful disposition of his heart. In regeneration and conversion man is made free in his will, but not entirely so. The Confessions cite Romans chapter 7 as a reminder of the conflict that continues in the believer. The fifth paragraph of the chapter on free will declares, 'It is not until man enters the state of glory that he is made perfectly and immutably free to will that which is good, and that alone.'[3]

Writing in 1957 in the introduction to a new translation of Luther's *Bondage of the Will*, J. I .Packer and O. R. Johnston wrote as follows: 'To accept the principles which Martin Luther vindicates in *The Bondage of the Will* would certainly involve a mental and spiritual revolution for many Christians at the present time. It would involve a radically different approach to preaching and the practice of evangelism, and to most other departments of theology and pastoral work as well. God-centred thinking is out of fashion today, and its recovery will involve something of a Copernican revolution in our outlook on many matters.'[4]

Is this an exaggeration? Not at all, because wrong doctrine leads to erroneous practice. From a correct or erroneous conception of man's ability in the matter of salvation proceeds either a correct or erroneous method of gospel preaching, together with right or wrong practices in the churches.

When the reality of sin and its radical effects on the whole man are bypassed the idea takes over that it simply takes a decision for Christ to bring about the new birth. A decision for Christ is all that is needed. This is 'easy-believism', in which repentance from sin is sidelined. Those who make a decision receive a pronouncement that they are saved. This proves premature. False converts are the outcome. The theory of the carnal Christian has been invented in order to accommodate those who have made a decision but who bear no marks of the new birth. *Are You Really Born Again?* by Kent Philpott[5] is a powerful contemporary book which describes and illustrates with many examples the damage done by misguided methods which stem from an inadequate view of man in sin. The appeal, or altar call, is the device most commonly used to exert psychological pressure in order to induce decisions.[6] The outcome is seen in the fact that the back door to some churches proves as large as the front door. In other words, many come in, make decisions, yet are not changed, not born again, and leave by the back door disillusioned.

2. Wrong thinking about God's sovereignty

The second set of wrong conclusions referred to above concerns muddled thinking about the sovereignty of God. The areas here which need clarification concern fatalism, the free offers of the gospel and the extent of God's love towards mankind.

Firstly, with regard to *fatalism*, the Puritans countered this mind-set by concentrating on what we call 'the means of grace'. On the subject of saving faith, the Confessions teach that this is wrought by the Holy Spirit through the preaching of the Word. The book of Acts illustrates well that the church grew and spread through the active efforts of the apostles and believers. Organized evangelism and enterprise in missions are the responsibility of every church and without such effort there will be no growth. A sovereign God achieves his purpose through the work of his people.

In addition to the above there is also the responsibility of sinners. God commands all people everywhere to repent (Acts 17:30). 'And this is his command: to believe in the name of his Son, Jesus Christ' (1 John 3:23). A sermon by William Greenhill, 'What must and can persons do toward their own conversion?' describes the responsibilities of the unconverted person.[7] Greenhill takes as his text Ezekiel 18:32 (AV): 'Wherefore turn yourselves, and live ye.' The unconverted may sit under a powerful ministry; they may listen to the voice of God's judgements; they may observe the difference the gospel has made in the lives of Christians. These are among the suggestions of what *may* be done. Greenhill then presses what the unconverted person *must* do. He must turn to God. He must strive to enter in at the narrow gate.

Secondly, with regard to *the free offers of the gospel*, the Puritans were not inhibited in the way they addressed the unconverted. Examples are Richard Baxter's *A Call to the Unconverted* and Joseph Alleine's *An Alarm to the Unconverted.* Baxter's *Call* is a classic and a modern English version of it is now available, prepared by John Blanchard.[8] The Puritans regarded all preaching as evangelistic, sometimes more and sometimes less so, depending on the subject in hand. The Lord Jesus Christ, said Robert Bolton, is 'offered most freely, and without exception of any person, every Sabbath, every sermon, either in plain, and direct terms, or implied, at the least'.[9] John Flavel's 265-page exposition of Revelation 3:20[10] well illustrates the unction of the Puritans in pressing home the gospel to all without exception. Sinners are to be invited to come to Christ (Matt. 11:27-28), reasoned with (Isa. 1:18-20), persevered with (Rom. 10:21), warned (Luke 13:5) and implored to be reconciled to God (2 Cor. 5:20).[11]

In the Puritan tradition George Whitefield wonderfully exemplified in his preaching a stable understanding of divine sovereignty and human responsibility. He used to place lost sinners in a vice. He pressed home the necessity of repentance. But the lost sinner is a slave. He cannot repent. Yet to be saved he must repent. He cannot. He must. His only recourse is to look away from himself to the one who can save. His escape route is cut off. There is no help in himself. His only hope is to call on God for mercy. And a God of mercy will never cast out those who come to him in faith.

Thirdly, there is the question of *God's love*. If God only loves the elect and has only hatred for the non-elect what constraint is there for the sinner to turn and believe? Richard Baxter, in his *Call to the Unconverted*, drives home the strong language and reasoning used by the Sovereign Lord as expressed in Ezekiel 33:11: 'He has no pleasure in the wicked that he should die, but rather that his pleasure is that the wicked person should turn from his wicked way and live.' Our Lord made it clear that we are to love our enemies because God loves them (Luke 6:35).[12] The love of God for all mankind, even for the most terrible sinners, is well expressed by the Puritan John Howe in his sermon, 'The Redeemer's tears shed over lost souls'.[13]

Conclusion

The Puritans were blessed with a stable doctrine of divine sovereignty and human responsibility. This enabled them to persevere in their work knowing that in spite of the discouragements a harvest would be reaped. In our time there is so much that seems impervious to the gospel. We too need a stable doctrine in which we trust in God's sovereign power to give the increase but at the same time know that persevering labour is imperative. Like the sower in the parable (Luke 8:1-15) we must sow the seed knowing that there will be a harvest in due course.

when the reality of sin and its radical effects on the whole man are bypassed the idea takes over that it simply takes a decision for Christ to bring about the new birth.

3.
The recovery of the Lord's Day

The battle for the Lord's Day was initiated towards the end of Elizabeth's reign and was won decisively during the first half of the seventeenth century. The Puritans gave England the English Sunday. The advantages of a whole day set apart for worship and fellowship were immense.[1]

D. L. Moody was not in the Puritan tradition but I quote him as a pointer to illustrate the practical importance of this issue today. He said, 'You show me a nation that has given up the Sabbath and I will show you a nation that has got the seeds of decay.' And to quote an enemy of the gospel, Voltaire declared, 'If you want to kill Christianity you must abolish Sunday.'[2] The restoration of a Christianity in decline will go hand in hand with the restoration of the Lord's Day.

'The essence of this early Puritan Sabbatarianism', maintains Patrick Collinson, 'was the conviction that the fourth commandment is a perpetual moral law originating with the creation and antedating the Mosaic law. Recognition of Sunday as the Christian Sabbath was reputed to be of divine and apostolic appointment, not ecclesiastical tradition. Sabbatarianism also entailed the conviction that the entire day had to be set aside for the public and private exercise of religion, with no time devoted to labour, idleness, or recreation.'[3]

We may be tempted to think that observance of the Lord's Day in Western society has declined to such an extent that it will never be recovered to its former position. Richard Baxter recalled his childhood experience in an English village when 'We could not on the Lord's Day either read a chapter, or pray, or sing a psalm, or catechise or instruct a servant, for the noise of the piper and tabor, and shouting in the streets, continually in our ears, and we were the common scorn of all the rabble in the streets, and we were called Puritans, precisionists, hypocrites because we rather chose on the Lord's Day to read the Scriptures rather than what they did.'[4] A great change came about. How did that reformation take place?

The story of the change can be traced to Richard Greenham, who influenced his son-in-law, Nicholas Bownde. Bownde preached on the subject of the Sabbath in 1586. He then marshalled the Sabbath-law arguments in a book which he published in 1595. This was a straightforward and balanced work on the text of the Fourth Commandment. It became enormously influential, appearing in an expanded edition in 1606. According to historian Daniel Neal, 'A mighty reformation was wrought.'[5]

Bownde proclaimed that the commandment to rest was a moral and perpetually binding law. To follow studies, do worldly business or engage in recreations or pleasures such as shooting, hawking, tennis playing, fencing and bowling was discouraged. 'Men must not come to church with their bows and arrows.'[6]

Bownde's brother-in-law, John Dod, nicknamed John Decalogue Dod, published his work on the Ten Commandments later. The book was very popular, going to forty editions. Concerning harvesting on Sunday Dod wrote, '"What about reaping our harvests endangered by ill weather?" ask some. "Trust in providence" is the reply. Better we hazard some part of our estate than the wrath of God fall on us.'

Two members of the Westminster Assembly, Daniel Cawdrey and Herbert Palmer, collaborated to produce *Sabbatum Redivivum — The Christian Sabbath Vindicated* (1645). In two volumes this work came to 1050 pages. The authors begin by establishing the distinction between ceremonial, judicial and moral law, and early define what they mean by 'moral'. Solemn worship they uphold as a moral and perpetual obligation. The Decalogue represents the summary, both Godward and manward, of perpetual and moral obligation. The Fourth Commandment, being part of the first table, they assert as being moral and perpetual. In 1655 a significant work by Thomas Shepard, the New England Puritan, was published. Shepard expounds the morality, change of day, beginning of, and sanctification of, the Sabbath.

In 1668 *The Practical Sabbatarian* appeared. This was a 787-page exposition of instructions on the duties of Sabbath observance written by John Wells of St Olave Jewry, London. Wells was one of the ministers ejected in 1662. His work is an exposition of Isaiah 58:13-14. He contends that sports and recreation on the Lord's Day easily remove the sweetness of the Word and are the debasements of spiritual mercies. The law of nature requires a total abstinence from all works of labour and pleasure during the time allotted and consecrated to God's service (pp.26-8). The very essence of the day, argues Wells, is apartness, or holiness, from the other days: 'Shall men fix days for themselves,' he asks 'and shall not God have one?' We must prepare for this day: 'Was not Mary Magdalene last at the cross and first at the sepulchre?' (p.241). And then he stresses the delight of the Lord's Day: 'Joy suits no person so much as the saint and no day so well as the Sabbath' (p.267). In support he quotes Psalm 118:24 (AV): 'This is the day which the Lord hath made; we will rejoice and be glad in it.' Between morning and evening service he advises that we indulge in 'luscious, sweet, holy discourse' (p.320).

A typical outline of advice would run as follows:

> 1. Prepare well for the Lord's Day by prayer and meditation. 'If you would leave your heart with God on the Saturday night,' says Swinnock, 'you should find it with him on the Lord's Day morning,' 'Go seasonably to bed so that you may not be sleepy on the Lord's Day.'
> 2. Heads of homes should gather their families in good time on Sunday mornings and prepare them all to receive maximum spiritual edification throughout the day. Public worship is central on the Lord's Day.
> 3. Heads of families should make sure that the sermon materials are retained. Encourage lively discussion and repetition of the main heads of the exposition at the meal table.
> 4. Seek to retain the teachings received and the blessings of the Lord's Day during the week that has begun.[7]

It is misguided to think that Puritan teaching on the Lord's Day is only negative. It is negative in the sense that we must forsake pleasing ourselves and rather seek the Lord's will for the best use of his day, but the power of Puritan teaching lies in its expressions of enjoyment of, and zeal for, the Lord's Day. The advantages of this day well spent are enormous. Thomas Watson calls it 'the market-day of the soul' and we can see from the following quotations the zeal that Watson felt for the Lord's Day:

> The Sabbath is the market-day of the soul, the cream of time. It is the day of Christ's rising from the grave, and the Holy Ghost's descending upon the earth. It is perfumed with the sweet odour of prayer, which goes up to heaven as incense. On this day the manna falls, that is, angels' food. This is the soul's festival day, on which the graces act their part: the other days of the week are most employed about earth, this day about heaven; then you gather straw, now pearls. Now Christ takes the soul up into the mount, and gives it transfiguring sights of glory. Now he leads his spouse into the wine-cellar, and displays the banner of his love. Now he gives her his spiced wine, and the juice of the pomegranate (S. of S. 2:4; 8:2).
>
> The Lord usually reveals himself more to the soul on this day. The apostle John was in the Spirit on the Lord's Day (Rev. 1:10). He was carried up on this day in divine raptures toward heaven. This day a Christian is in the heights; he walks with God and takes as it were a turn with him in heaven (1 John 1:3). On this day holy affections are quickened; the stock of grace is improved; corruptions are weakened; and Satan falls like lightning before the majesty of the Word. Christ wrought most of his miracles upon the Sabbath; so he does still: dead souls are raised and hearts of stone are made flesh. How highly should we esteem and reverence this day! It is more precious than rubies. God has anointed it with the oil of gladness above its fellows. On the Sabbath we are doing angels' work. Our tongues are tuned to God's praises. The Sabbath on earth is a shadow and type of the glorious rest and eternal Sabbath we hope for in heaven, when God shall be the temple, and the Lamb shall be the light of it (Rev. 21:22-23).[8]

4.
Marriage and the family

The statistics for the breakdown of family life in Britain and America are startling. In America thirty-one per cent of children are born to parents who were never married. Over fifty per cent of couples live together before marriage. Sixty per cent of marriages fail, fifty per cent ending in divorce and ten per cent in separation. Those who have sex before marriage have a sixty per cent higher divorce rate than those who do not.[1]

Against this dark background we have much to learn from the Puritans. 'Under God,' suggests Dr Packer, 'they were creators of the English Christian marriage, the English Christian family, and the English Christian home.'[2] 'The Puritan ethic of marriage was to look not for a partner whom you do love passionately at this moment, but rather for one whom you can love steadily as your best friend for life, and then to proceed with God's help to do just that.' The Puritan ethic of nurture was to train up children in the way they should go, to care for their bodies and souls together, and to educate them for sober, godly, socially useful adult living. The Puritan way of home life was based on maintaining order, courtesy and family worship. Goodwill, patience, consistency and an encouraging attitude were seen as the essential domestic virtues.

William Gouge preached on marriage and the family and wrote a treatise of over 600 pages on this theme.[3] Thomas Manton preached thirty-two consecutive sermons on Ephesians 5:1-27.[4] Following on in the footsteps of the Puritans, Dr Martyn Lloyd-Jones expounded Ephesians 5:1-27 at Westminster Chapel on Sunday mornings during 1959 and 1960 and this material was later published in a series of volumes.[5]

The aptitude and readiness to preach on the practical aspects of marriage and the family is seen in some of the famous sermons published under the title of *The Morning Exercises at Cripplegate*. For example, Richard Adams preached on, 'What are the duties of parents and children and how are they to be managed according to Scripture?' and, 'How may child-bearing women be most encouraged and supported against, in, and under the hazard of their travail?'

We should remember that Puritan teaching on marriage and the family was in stark contrast with centuries of Roman Catholic tradition. It was a major break with the medieval idea that celibacy is the best way to holiness when Martin Luther married ex-nun Katherine von Bora. The Puritans carried forward the example begun by the sixteenth-century Reformers and went forward to expound in more detail the biblical passages relating to husbands and wives and the family. In so doing they taught that marriage was not God's second best but his very best. For instance, Thomas Gataker extolled marriage thus: 'There is no society more near, more entire, more needful, more kindly, more delightful, more comfortable, more constant, more continual, than the society of man and wife, the main root, source, and original of all other societies.'[6] Thomas Manton declared that marriages are made in heaven before they are made on earth,[7] and George Swinnock, on 'The exercise of godliness in the relationship of husbands and wives', points out that 'Adam was married to Eve before he broke his covenant with his God. He was married to a wife before he was marred by the wicked one. Surely those popish doctors who term it filthiness and pollution do not consider that it was ordained before man's fall and corruption.'[8] And on this theme Richard Sibbes declared, 'It was the Devil that brought in a base esteem of that honourable condition.'[9]

Thomas Manton raises marriage to the highest conceivable level when he expounds the text, 'Husbands, love your wives, just as Christ loved the church and gave himself up for her' (Eph. 5:25). He cites Luther's words, 'I see nothing in Christ but a prodigality and excess of love,' and endorses that by saying, 'Love will in time beget love, as fire kindleth fire,' and affirming with 1 John 4:19 that 'We love him because he first loved us.'

The paragraphs in *The Westminster Confession* on marriage stipulate that Christians are to marry only 'in the Lord'. In listing reasons for marriage, 'mutual help of husband and wife' are placed first and 'the increase of mankind' second.

Family worship was regarded as a vital daily duty and took place morning and evening. Children were brought up in the fear and nurture of the Lord. The advantages of a thorough knowledge of Scripture from an early age are illustrated by the example of Matthew Henry, son of the Puritan Philip Henry, who from childhood imbibed a living and amazing knowledge of Scripture. This enabled him later to write his wonderful commentary on the whole Bible which continues to be in demand. In his commentary on Genesis 2:22 Matthew Henry comments on the relationship of the man to the woman: 'The woman was made of a rib out of the side of Adam; not made out of his head to top him, nor out of his feet to be trampled on by him, but out of his side to be equal with him, under his arm to be protected, and near his heart to be loved by him.'

Matthew Henry's commentary on Proverbs 31:10-31 shows that all the duties of the home are pleasing to God. Grace permeates the whole of life and inspires all living. Grace, or spirituality, is not against nature, or above it, or even alongside it, but rather permeates it. The Puritans stressed that marriage was essentially a partnership. Samuel Sewall in his diary records that the family finances were delegated to his wife for the reason that she had 'a better faculty than I for managing affairs'.[10]

The Puritans taught that every physical and spiritual provision was to be made for children, including instruction 'in some honest lawful calling, labour or employment, either in husbandry, or in some other trade profitable for themselves and the commonwealth'.[11] With regard to discipline, Richard Greenham counselled that it be exercised with 'the mildest means and with the least rigour'.[12]

Since about the 1960s a massive spiritual attack has been made on the Christian view of marriage and the family. The constant stream of anti-Christian propaganda from the mass media can be countered with biblical teaching with special emphasis on practical application. The Puritans set a good example by applying their minds to this subject and expounding it with clear applications. Pastors should preach regularly in a lively and practical way on the relevant passages of Scripture on marriage and the family. Richard Baxter preached and wrote evangelistically on the subject of marriage and the family.[13] He taught that the Christian family is a role model for society. In the Christian family we can see the work of Christ in action visibly. This is tremendously relevant today. In a world in which many leaders who have a high profile set an appalling example, Christians should set a godly example in their family lives.

5.
A biblical basis for spiritual experience

Behind the drugs and sex revolution of the 1960s lies the driving desire for experience. The spirit of the world has flooded into the churches and that spirit is the spirit of postmodernism in which what people feel is esteemed as paramount. If it feels right it must be right! Since the 1970s the influence of the charismatic movement has escalated and during the 1990s the experience called the Toronto Blessing was widely acclaimed although many, including numbers in Pentecostal churches, rejected the type of experiences associated with the Toronto Blessing as fanatical and unbiblical. The Toronto Blessing manifestations have included all kinds of wild behaviour. Doctors have diagnosed these excesses and described them as epidemic hysteria.[1]

The subject of spiritual experience is at the forefront of thinking in evangelicalism worldwide today. A clear line of division can be drawn between those who insist that the Bible must be the basis by which all spiritual experience is tested and those who regard experience as pre-eminent and resist the tests of Scripture. Is the Word our authority, or is spiritual experience our authority? The Puritans were strong in the area of knowing God by heart experience but they sought to test everything by Scripture. We do well to follow their example.

What do we understand by experience? Experience is what I feel in my soul. Experience has to do with my emotional life. Christianity is a religion of the intellect and the heart and practice. Experience has its rightful place. Christianity is a 'felt' religion. Paul says that 'God has poured out his love into our hearts by the Holy Spirit, whom he has given us' (Rom. 5:5). We understand Pentecost to have been a time of intense spiritual experience. The disciples were filled with the Holy Spirit. Their hearts and minds were greatly empowered.

There is a tendency to think of experience exclusively in terms of the sensational. The Day of Pentecost is one example of this. Isaiah's experience of being overwhelmed by the glory and majesty of God in the temple is another (Isa. 6:1-6). Such spectacular experiences are few and far between. For instance, John Flavel describes how, on a journey by horseback, his 'thoughts began to swell, and rise higher and higher, like the waters in Ezekiel's vision, till at last they became an overflowing flood'. He came to a spring where he sat down and washed and earnestly desired that he might die, but having drunk of the spring, he felt revived and continued his journey. He came to an inn where he spent the night but did not sleep at all, though he never had a sweeter night's rest in all his life! Still the joy of the Lord overwhelmed him, and he seemed to be an inhabitant of another world! Many years later he called that day 'one of the days of heaven on earth', and professed he understood more of the light of heaven by it than by all the books he ever read, or discourses he had entertained about it.[2]

In their thinking the Puritans did not confine experience to extraordinary occasions like this one described by Flavel, nor did they think in terms of a second mandatory experience called the baptism of the Spirit. Rather they viewed spiritual experience along the lines of the Psalms, which describe the whole range of experiences, the highs and lows, the exquisite joys as well as the desperate depressions of the soul.

Later in the Puritan tradition Jonathan Edwards (1703-1758) wrote his classic work *The Religious Affections,* probably the most penetrating analysis of Christian inward experience ever written.[3] Edwards commences his work with an exposition of 1 Peter 1:8: 'Though you have not seen him, you love him; and even though you do not see him now, you believe in him and are filled with an inexpressible and glorious joy.' 'True religion', suggests Edwards, 'in great part consists in holy affections,' by which he means the experience of the heart; in other words, a felt religion.[4]

The Puritan writers addressed every kind of spiritual experience: joy, love, depression, desertion, tribulation, conflict, contentment and chastening.[5] Foundational to all experience is the believer's experience of union and communion with God. Beginning with an exposition of 1 John 1:3, John Owen explains that communion is with each person of the Godhead individually.[6] In communion with the Father, Owen suggests that 'The chief way by which the saints have communion with the Father is love — free, undeserved, eternal love.' The glories and excellencies of Christ are unfolded and the believer is encouraged to deepen his experience of union and communion with Christ. Owen explains the ways in which we have communion with the Holy Spirit. He is very practical and explains how we can enjoy such fellowship.

'Delighting in God', an exposition of Psalm 37:4, 'Delight yourself in the Lord, and he will give you the desires of your heart,' by John Howe[7] is an outstanding example of Puritan exposition of Christian experience: 'God's pleasure is that he himself would be the great object of his people's delight.'

Stress on meaningful, rich fellowship with the three persons of the Godhead is never far away in Puritan exposition. For instance, Thomas Brooks takes as his text Lamentations 3:24 (AV): 'The LORD is my portion, saith my soul; therefore will I hope in him.' Brooks calls his theme: 'An ark for all God's Noahs'.[8] He divides the text as follows:

> *First,* an assertion: 'The LORD is my portion.'
> *Second,* a proof of it in those words: 'Saith my soul'.
> *Third,* the inference from these premises: 'Therefore will I hope in him.'

Brooks reminds us that the relevance of this for Christian experience lies in the context. The Israelites had lost everything: 'Grievous calamities and miseries had befallen the Jews.' 'The prophet bewails the ruin of their state, the devastation of their land, the destruction of their glorious city and temple.' The reasoning is that when a believer has lost everything and stands amidst the ruins of this world, he has the Lord as his portion. If he has the Lord, he has everything.

What kind of portion is Jehovah? Brooks expounds what it means in experimental terms to have our God as a present portion. He is with us now! He is immense. He is all-sufficient. He is glorious, happy and blessed. He is soul-satisfying. He is incomparable. These are some of the fifteen aspects of the Lord's character brought out by Brooks in his examination of this passage.

An outstanding example of Bible-based experimental exposition is found in the book on the work of Christ by Isaac Ambrose. Born in 1591, Ambrose settled in Lancashire. He was among the ejected clergy in 1662. As he recovered from a severe illness, he experienced a lively sense of what Jesus had done for his soul. He was gripped by a desire to reciprocate Christ's love and express this by way of expositions of the life of Christ. A classic work of 700 pages, with the title *Looking unto Jesus*, was the outcome.

What is it to look unto Jesus? First, we must look to him in each phase of his life and ministry, from his pre-existence to his conception, his birth, and then through each year of his ministry, his rejection and suffering, his crucifixion, resurrection, ascension, exaltation and present ministry of intercession for us. At each point Ambrose requires that we consider Jesus, desire him, hope in him, believe in him, love him, joy in him, call on him and conform to him.

The subject of experience is closely joined to that of assurance of salvation. Thomas Brooks declares, 'Assurance will give you a possession of heaven,' and 'An assured soul lives in paradise, and walks in paradise, and works in paradise, and rests in paradise; he hath heaven within him and heaven about him, and heaven over him.'[9]

6.
A robust doctrine of assurance

Heaven on Earth is the title given by Thomas Brooks to his famous treatise on the subject of Christian assurance.[1]

> To be in a state of grace is to be miserable no more; it is to be happy for ever. Now assurance is a reflex act of a gracious soul, whereby he clearly and evidently sees himself in a gracious, blessed, and happy state; it is a sensible feeling, and an experimental discerning of a man's being in a state of grace, and of having a right to a crown of glory; and this rises from the seeing in himself the special, peculiar, and distinguishing graces of Christ, or from the testimony and report of the Spirit of God, 'the Spirit bearing witness with his spirit, that he is a son, and an heir-apparent of glory' (Rom. 8:16-17).
>
> It is one thing for me to have grace, it is another thing for me to see my grace... Now this assurance is the beauty ... of a Christian's glory in this life. It is usually attended with the strongest joy, with the sweetest comforts, and with the greatest peace. Assurance is not of the essence of a Christian. It is required to the *bene esse* [the well-being], to the comfortable and joyful being of a Christian; but it is not required to the *esse*, to the being of a Christian. A man may be a true believer, and yet would give all the world ... to know that he is a believer.[2]

Thomas Brooks unfolds what he terms 'the things that accompany salvation', namely faith, repentance, obedience, love, prayer, perseverance and hope. In a manner typical of the Puritans, he unites the direct witness of the Holy Spirit — 'The Spirit himself testifies with our spirit that we are God's children' (Rom. 8:16) — with inferred or deduced assurance. The Holy Spirit who gives spiritual life enables the believer to recognize that spiritual life. Thus, in his first epistle, John speaks of the direct witness of the Holy Spirit: 'And this is how we know that he lives in us: we know it by the Spirit he gave us' (1 John 3:24). But John at the same time gives tests for assurance: the three tests known as the doctrinal test, the moral test and the social test. I know that I have eternal life because I believe that Jesus is the Son of God (1 John 5:1); I love God and carry out his commands (1 John 5:3); and 'We know that we have passed from death to life because we love our brothers' (1 John 3:14). There must be no conflict between direct and inferred assurance. The Holy Spirit who assures me directly in my heart that I am a child of God is the same Spirit who has worked new life in my heart and conduct. The two go together and complement each other.

At least twenty-five members of the Westminster Assembly had written treatises relating to faith and assurance prior to the Assembly. The sixteenth-century Reformers virtually equated faith with assurance but, as we see from the passage quoted above from Brooks, the Puritans made a clear distinction between the two. Saving faith and assurance must be distinguished.

The Puritan doctrine of assurance is formally outlined in chapter 18 of *The Westminster Confession.*[3] The subject is addressed in four paragraphs: first, the possibility of assurance; secondly, the foundation of assurance; thirdly, the cultivation of assurance; and, fourthly, the renewal of assurance. Of these paragraphs the second is the most important as assurance is united on three bases: first, the subjective base of the objective reality of the Word of God with its promises to those who believe; second, the subjective basis of inward evidence; and, third, the subjective testimony of the Spirit of adoption witnessing with our spirits.

The way in which the Puritans expounded assurance is highly relevant in today's evangelical climate.

An outstanding feature in Puritan theology was the ability to distinguish principles and hold these in tension, or balance. An example, as we have seen, is divine sovereignty and human responsibility. Another is the warrant of faith and the way to faith. In this question of assurance the Puritans distinguished between direct assurance and inferred or deduced assurance and would not allow any conflict between the two. The same Holy Spirit who assures directly in the heart — 'The Spirit himself testifies with our spirit that we are God's children' (Rom. 8:16) — also enables believers to live the life of faith and produces fruit in their lives. The stronger the spiritual life in practice, the more likely the direct witness of the Spirit in the heart will be.

How do we deal with the objection that exhorting the believer to look for his assurance to his life of loving fellow-Christians and obeying God's precepts tends to legalism and to self-righteousness? The answer is that it is the Holy Spirit who enables Christians to do good works, so that we never esteem our good works to be the basis of our justification. We rest only on the righteousness of Christ imputed to us. Christ our righteousness is our only justification. Yet it is imperative to our assurance that we evidence our reciprocal love to Christ which is expressed in obeying his commands.

Brooks' counsel to believers as to ways and means of gaining a well-grounded assurance is as follows: be active in exercising grace; follow the path of obedience; follow diligently the instructions of the Holy Spirit; be diligent in attendance upon ordinances; pay particular attention to the scope of God's promises of mercy; distinguish those matters in which believers are different from all others; seek to grow in grace; seek assurance when the soul is in its best frame (that is, when it is well-grounded); ascertain whether you have the things which accompany salvation (knowledge, faith, repentance, obedience, love, prayer, perseverance and hope).

It is possible to lose assurance and suffer much conflict of soul as a result. Brooks suggests six methods whereby souls who have lost assurance may be kept from fainting, and offers five suggestions whereby they may recover it. One source of encouragement for the person exercised over the matter of lost assurance is to remember that eternal happiness does not depend upon assurance; another is that though assurance may be lost, 'blessed breathings and sweet influences of the Spirit upon them' are not lost. 'Witness', he says, 'their love to Christ, their longing after Christ, their fear of offending Christ, their care to please Christ.'

While I agree with Brooks in most of his exposition, I cannot concur with him on the idea that God sometimes takes away assurance. For instance, Job experienced the most acute sense of desertion (which is expressed in Job 23:8-10; 30:9-19), yet he always possessed the strongest assurance and could say, 'I know that my Redeemer lives, and that in the end he will stand upon the earth' (Job 19:25). We should always think in terms of God's giving assurance and not confuse loss of assurance with desertion, to which we now give our attention.

Wherever shallow evangelism, with its practice of calling for 'decisions', has prevailed, the danger exists of a false assurance of salvation. Connected to this kind of evangelism is the 'lordship' controversy. A number of books have appeared recently on this theme.[4] In order to include those who have made a profession of faith but show no spiritual progress, the idea has been promoted that as long as a person has made a decision for Christ he is saved. Even though that person has not received Christ as Lord and shows no spiritual life he or she is still to be esteemed a Christian. But the Scripture declares, 'Without holiness no one will see the Lord' (Heb. 12:14). How does a person know that he is saved? If he claims that he has a strong inward feeling and calls this the Spirit witnessing with his spirit that he is a Christian, yet at the same time lacks a credible Christian life, we may conclude that he is deceiving himself. The message of the first epistle of John provides adequate material to prove that a Christian lifestyle is essential for a well-grounded assurance.

Although it was written in the mid-seventeenth century, I know of no better, clearer or more relevant book on assurance than Brooks' *Heaven on Earth*.

7.
Hope for the future of the church

As we enter the third millennium, the foremost issue facing the church is the completion of the great mandate to take the gospel to all nations. In China, Africa and Central and South America there has been rapid growth during the twentieth century. Will the gospel continue to spread until the whole world is filled with the truth of Scripture? The Puritans were optimistic.[1]

Question 191 of the *Larger Westminster Catechism* sums up the Puritan view:

> *Question:* What do we pray for in the second petition of the Lord's prayer?
> *Answer:* We pray that the kingdom of sin and Satan may be destroyed, the gospel propagated throughout the world, the Jews called and the fulness of the Gentiles be brought in.

This answer expresses the programme of God for the nations. Foundational to the sovereign programme of the Father is the exaltation of Jesus. In his exposition of Psalm 110 Edward Reynolds (1593-1676) observes that 'This reign at the right hand of the majesty and glory signifies to us the great exaltation of the Lord Christ.'[2]

The Puritans varied in their views of prophecy but the majority believed that the cause of Christ would be victorious in the world.[3] Psalm 110:1 describes the throne from which Christ initiates and pursues his conquest:

> The LORD says to my Lord;
> 'Sit at my right hand
> until I make your enemies
> a footstool for your feet.'

Puritan expositors such as Reynolds, Matthew Henry and Matthew Poole subscribed to the following principles:

1. There will be one final period known as the last days from the first to the second advent of Christ.
2. Christ will employ his power increasingly during that time to subdue his enemies.
3. Christ's power is exerted to subdue his enemies in order that his kingdom can extend and his church be built among all nations.
4. This will be accompanied by conflict. Psalm 110:1 is the most quoted Old Testament text in the New Testament. In 1 Corinthians 15:25 Paul declares that Christ must reign at the Father's right hand until he has put all his enemies under his feet. The last enemy to be destroyed is death.

The second principle stated above concerns the enemies of Christ. These include powers of evil and apostasy that have worked in the church to destroy it. The most telling passage concerning the man of sin is commonly termed the 'little apocalypse' of 2 Thessalonians 2:1-12. Thomas Manton expounds these verses in ten sermons.[4] He demonstrates that the apostasy described by Paul is an apostasy from apostolic Christianity which took place over the centuries and is seen in the development of the Roman Catholic Church and the papacy which usurped the gospel. This was the teaching of mainline Puritanism and is enshrined in *The Westminster Confession of Faith*.

John Calvin interprets the passage as apocalyptic in style and not literal. Concerning the man of sin, he says, 'Paul is not speaking of one individual, but of a kingdom that was to be seized by Satan for the purpose of setting up a seat of abomination in the midst of God's temple. This we see accomplished in popery.' Speaking of the Antichrist, Calvin asserts, 'For quite certainly Paul meant that Antichrist would seize the things which belong to God alone, his purpose being to exalt himself above every divine power, so that all religion and all worship of God should lie beneath his feet.' This interpretation is followed by John Owen.[5] No apostasy from apostolic Christianity can be compared to the papacy. For over a thousand years the gospel became more and more subverted and covered over with error. The church became the monolithic, institutionalized persecutor of the faithful in the name of religion, driving them to death or into the wilderness, as described in Revelation chapter 12.

If texts which describe Antichrist are taken out of context then the future is one of fearful doom and gloom. However, if these texts are taken as warnings within the framework of God's overall purpose and within the context of the advance of the gospel worldwide, we may be more optimistic. Two principles are working side by side. The first is that evil-doers will get worse and worse. We see this in drug traffic and the Mafia and in vastly corrupt civil governments as well as in the landslide of personal morality. The second is that in spite of huge opposition our Lord will have the victory over his enemies and will not return until they have become his footstool (1 Cor. 15:25).

The third principle summarized above is that the gospel will triumph throughout the world. The glory of Christ in the victories he is given for his holy gospel must be commensurate with the horrendous nature of his sufferings. His reward is described in Psalm 22:27-31 and Isaiah 49:1-7. The salvation he brings will not be in a corner. His salvation will go to the ends of the earth. Kings will acknowledge the glory of Christ. This will be through the prayers and efforts of his people. Psalm 2 urges prayer that the nations be given to Christ and the uttermost parts of the earth become his possession. His kingdom 'will crush all those kingdoms and bring them to an end, but it will itself endure for ever' (Dan. 2:44). The stone that struck the feet of the image itself grows and fills the whole earth (Dan. 2:35).

Many other passages run parallel to this theme, such as Isaiah chapters 2, 11, 60 and 61. John Howe, in an exposition entitled 'The Prosperous State of the Christian Interest before the End of Time, by a Plentiful Effusion of the Holy Spirit', takes as his text Isaiah 2:2 and makes it clear that he understands that 'in the latter part of the latter time' there will be a great outpouring of the Holy Spirit resulting in a cessation of wars — 'such a time as the world hath not yet known'.[6] Psalm 72 confirms that the whole earth is to be filled with the glory of the Lord as the waters cover the sea. Psalm 72 and Isaiah 64 provide models as to how we are to pray for this to take place. These are not descriptions of heaven but rather prayers which involve terrific conflict and the struggle for justice and the relief of the oppressed.

Elnathan Parr exercised a powerful ministry at Palgrave in Suffolk. In his commentary on Romans 11 Parr develops the contrast between the Jews and Gentiles. 'The casting off of the Jews was our calling but the calling of the Jews shall not be our casting off but our greater enriching in grace.'[7] On verse 15, 'For if their rejection is the reconciliation of the world, what will their acceptance be but life from the dead?' Parr suggests that 'The calling of the Jews seems a thing impossible, yet it is not so to God, who can as easily call them to Christ as raise the dead.' 'Here we are put in mind to pray for the Jews.' Life from the dead, Parr suggests, is revival, life, vigour, vivacity. Commenting on verse 25, 'And so all Israel will be saved,' Parr writes, 'Before the end of the world, the Jews, in regard to their multitude shall be called.' 'The calling of the Jews is a mystery. If you ask how and when I know not.' Parr interprets 'the fulness of the Gentiles' as 'a full and plentiful propagation of the gospel whereby many of all of the nations shall be converted to God'. Parr suggests, as do a number of modern commentators on Romans 11, that the comparison of Jews and Gentiles is sustained throughout the passage, and this argument is irresistible.[8]

The Puritan doctrine of the last things is a doctrine which inspires prayer, motivates effort, inculcates endurance and strengthens patience. Battles may be lost, but there is absolutely no doubt about who will win this war! It is this view of the promises of Scripture which inspired and motivated the pioneer missionaries such as William Carey, Adoniram Judson and Henry Martyn. One of the first to implement this outlook in missionary work was the Puritan John Eliot who in 1631, at the age of twenty-seven, sailed for Massachusetts. He became pastor of a new church a mile from Boston. Burdened for the Indian tribes, he set himself to master the Algonquin language. He began at the age of forty and eventually translated the entire Bible into Algonquin. Converts were made, churches planted and Indian pastors trained. By the time of his death, aged eighty-four, there were many Indian churches.

Surely, as has happened before, powerful forces of motivation and determination will be unleashed once the church grasps hold of the fact that it is truly our Father's intention and purpose to subdue and overcome all those systems of false religion arrayed against his Son. He urges in Psalm 2:

> Ask of me,
> and I will make the nations your inheritance,
> the ends of the earth your possession.

And through Malachi he declares, 'My name will be great among the nations, from the rising to the setting of the sun. In every place incense and pure offerings will be brought to my name, because my name will be great among the nations, says the LORD Almighty' (Mal. 1:11).

8.
The warrant of faith and the way to faith

Clarity in the distinction between the warrant of faith (i.e. what gives the sinner the right to believe in Christ for salvation) and the way to faith (i. e. how we are brought to saving faith) is vital to the Christian, and in this matter the Puritans can help us. I will approach this subject through Spurgeon, who loved the Puritans.

One of the famous sermons by Charles Haddon Spurgeon was called 'The Warrant of Faith'. This he preached on the morning of the Lord's Day, 20 September 1863 (the sermon being number 531 in the series that eventually reached 3,492). Spurgeon was only twenty-nine years old at the time. In this sermon he said:

> The warrant of our faith in Christ reasons thus: 'You are not saved by what you do but by what Christ did; but then you have no right to trust in Christ unless there is something good in you which shall entitle you to trust in him.' Now, this legal reasoning I oppose. I believe such teaching to contain in it the essence of popish self-righteousness. The warrant for a sinner to believe in Christ is not in himself in any sense or in any manner, but in the fact that he is commanded there and then to believe on Jesus Christ. Some preachers in the Puritanic times, whose shoe latchets I am not worthy to unloose, erred much in this matter. I refer not only to Alleine and Baxter, who are far better preachers of the law than of the gospel, but I include men far sounder in the faith than they, such as Rogers of Dedham, Shepherd, the author of *The Sound Believer*, and especially the American,

> Thomas Hooker, who has written a book upon qualifications for coming to Christ. These excellent men had a fear of preaching the gospel to any except those whom they styled 'sensible sinners', and consequently kept hundreds of their hearers sitting in darkness when they might have rejoiced in the light. They preached repentance and hatred of sin as the warrant of the sinner's trusting to Christ. According to them, a sinner might reason thus: 'I possess such-and-such a degree of sensibility on account of sin, therefore I have a right to trust in Christ.' Now, I venture to affirm that such reasoning is seasoned with fatal error.

Was the young Spurgeon right in his criticism of the Puritans? I would suggest that he is incorrect in this assessment because he himself was at fault in not making an adequate distinction between two vital principles, namely, the warrant of faith and the way of faith. I will explain this distinction in some detail, but at the outset will put it simply like this. If you are a parent, when you teach your children you read the Bible to them and teach them to read it. You pray with them and teach them to pray themselves. It may well be that, with countless other parents, you use a catechism and seek that they should benefit from that as it leads to further questions and answers and discussion. You may also sing with them and worship the Lord with them by way of singing. Yet you do not teach them that their doing these things earns them credit, nor that they *in themselves* have the right to come to God the Father through Jesus Christ for salvation. No, all these means form the *way to faith*, and that is a very different thing from the warrant of faith. The *warrant of faith* is God's command to all people everywhere to repent and believe solely on account of what he, the Almighty One, has provided in the great sacrifice of his Son.

When we read the Puritans, or any other body of worthy Bible expositors for that matter, we shall find frequent exhortations by them to attend to the ways by which faith comes: attend to preaching; mix with Christians; read your Bible; seek the Lord while he may be found; call on him while he is near. All these things form the way of faith, but they do not constitute the warrant of faith.

When the Philippian jailer cried out in an agony of conviction, 'What must I do to be saved?' the shortest, clearest and best answer was given: 'Believe in the Lord Jesus Christ and you will be saved.' Paul and Silas did not say, 'Go and read the prophet Isaiah and he will show you the way of salvation.' They did not say, 'Wait until next Lord's Day and go to church and you will be saved.' There is nothing wrong with counsel about the way of faith and what we need to do to get saving faith, but that counsel always needs to be given in the light of the warrant of faith, which is that God will always have all sinners to believe at once and to trust only in what he has provided for them in the person and work of his Son. Let us look more closely at the distinction between the warrant of faith and the way of faith.

What is the warrant of faith?

Webster's New Collegiate Dictionary gives six categories of usage for the noun 'warrant'. *The Oxford English Reference Dictionary* gives four, the first of which accurately describes the theological meaning we ascribe to the word 'warrant': 'anything that authorizes a person or an action'. For instance, in order for a police officer to arrest a person for an offence he needs to have a warrant authorizing his action. When we come to faith, what right does the sinner have to believe in Christ? The answer to that can be provided in the text: 'And this is [God's] command, to believe in the name of his Son, Jesus Christ' (1 John 3:23). The warrant is God's command that we believe, and nothing we do or feel in ourselves provides the warrant of faith. There is no merit of any kind whatsoever in us that gives us the right to believe. Rather, the fact that we are altogether sinful points to our need to repent and believe.

What is the way of faith?

There is a faith which is only nominal and there is also a faith which truly joins the sinner to Christ and which constitutes true saving faith. There is a kind of faith which is no more than intellectual assent. Multitudes today are led by the appeal system into the easy 'faith' of what is often called easy-believism, and thereby to the fatal peril of false assurance. That is misguided and cruel. We know from the Scriptures that we are always to encourage all sinners to believe, but if we are to be faithful to them we must first show them who Christ is, and how great their need is. We must not indulge in short cuts or over-simplifications. That is why we have to be careful about the way of faith.

The 'way of faith' is really the way to saving faith. That way comes by hearing the Word of God (Rom. 10:14). Hence we have to exhort unbelievers to hear and heed the Scriptures. With regard to that we can note passages like Proverbs 1:20-33 and 8:1-36. Wisdom personified, which we can take as representing Christ, pleads with all sinners everywhere to listen to instruction. Wisdom urges that we heed this counsel until our salvation is assured. Likewise in the great mandate of the free invitations and offers of the gospel contained in Isaiah 55 there is exhortation to listen, to hear, to seek, to call, to turn. Listening, hearing, seeking, calling, turning — all these are the way to faith, but in and of themselves they never form the warrant of faith.

Jesus dealt with Nicodemus by showing him the way of faith and that he was powerless to save himself. He told him to look to the serpent raised up on a stick and urged that he look outside himself to the Father's provision of salvation. Jesus did not try to rush him into something he did not yet understand; rather he guided him in the way of faith.

Likewise with the rich young ruler, Jesus showed him the way of faith by pointing him in the direction of learning the futility of his own riches. He told him to go home and sell all and then come to be a learner. That was pointing him to the way of faith. Jesus would fail the test of some of the Southern Baptist leaders who incessantly attempt to get people to make a profession of faith before such people know what faith is or the demands of the life of faith. Making a decision is one thing; the possession of a faith which unites the sinner to Christ for time and eternity is another. There must be care and prayer about teaching the way of faith.

Hence when the Puritans or other preachers urged the use of what we call 'the means of grace', they did not intend that those means were to be regarded as qualifications entitling a person to believe. They never taught that these means were to be esteemed as meritorious. Attending church, listening to preaching, reformation of life, self-examination in the light of the Ten Commandments, meditation on the coming great Judgement Day — these are all to do with the way in which a person is brought to faith in Christ. At the same time without intermission we always find in Puritan preaching the call of God to the immediate duty of repentance and faith, which in itself constitutes the warrant of faith.

Christian parents soon discover that it is impossible to create saving faith in their offspring. Only God can do that. A child can walk down the aisle and make a decision many times but that does not create saving faith. Yet godly parents never cease to urge their children to walk in the way of faith, that is, always to make use of the means of grace by which saving faith is bestowed by God.

Preparation on the way to saving faith

Before regenerating sinners, the Holy Spirit imparts knowledge. How can anyone believe unless he knows what to believe? In most cases the Holy Spirit engenders a conviction of sin and need, and sometimes he brings about a considerable degree of reformation of life on the part of the sinner even before the new birth takes place. Some have been known to quit blaspheming and to become truly attentive and serious about spiritual subjects before actually experiencing that great change we call the new birth. This preparatory work is known technically as 'prevenient grace' and sometimes it is referred to as preparation for conversion.

John Owen describes the preparation wrought by God in a soul prior to the new birth: 'There are certain *internal spiritual effects* wrought in and upon the souls of men, whereof the Word preached is the immediate instrumental cause, which ordinarily do precede the work of regeneration, of real conversion to God. And they are reducible unto three heads: 1. Illumination; 2. Conviction; 3. Reformation.' He then expounds these in detail.

If God prepares sinners for conversion what part are we to play to prepare them? The Puritans are sometimes charged with what is termed 'preparationism', by which is meant that instead of urging immediate repentance and faith in Christ to save they urge various duties, such as attending church, listening to preaching, reformation of life, self-examination in the light of the Ten Commandments and meditation on the coming great Judgement Day. But, as I have shown, there need not be a contradiction between, on the one hand, the way to faith (the fact that faith comes by hearing) and, on the other, the warrant of faith (the fact that there is always the immediate urgent command to believe and be saved).

Thomas Hooker was a Puritan who ministered in Chelmsford, Essex, where he exercised a powerful ministry. Cotton Mather declared that 'A great reformation was wrought, not only in the town but in the adjacent country, from all parts whereof they came "to hear the wisdom of the Lord Jesus Christ".'[1] In 1633, with 200 others, Hooker sailed to America. There he wrote the book *The Soul's Preparation for Christ.*[2] It is possible to criticize Hooker and accuse him of directing men more to their duties than to Christ. That is all very well, but the necessity of persevering in use of the means of grace applies to all, but especially those who have not as yet come to true saving faith in Christ, or who claim to have done so but show no evidence of the fruit of the Spirit and who may, therefore, be deceiving themselves. As long as we see that there is no contradiction whatsoever in, on the one hand, directing unsaved persons to attend to every means of grace that will enlighten and convict them and, on the other, holding firmly to the urgency of, and necessity for, repentance towards God and faith in the Lord Jesus Christ for immediate salvation, we shall avoid confusion. The way to faith and the warrant of faith to receive salvation at once are complementary, not contradictory.

It is possible to fall into the trap of thinking that a deep conviction of sin is what constitutes the right or warrant of faith. This can lead a person to think that it is no earthly use trusting in Christ for his salvation until he first has a previous deep conviction and sorrow for his sin. That is erroneous but, even if there were some truth in the idea it would tend to despair rather than encouraging faith, for who could ever tell whether he felt deep enough conviction or sufficient sorrow? If acceptance has to come by something we have to perform, or some quality in ourselves, then our position is hopeless.

The warrant of faith and the First London Confession

Paragraph 25 of *The First London Confession of Faith* of 1646 expresses clearly that the warrant of faith is God's command and lies in nothing we can do ourselves:

> The preaching of the gospel to the conversion of sinners is absolutely free; no way requiring as absolutely necessary any qualifications, preparations, or terrors of the law, or preceding ministry of the law, but only and alone the naked soul, a sinner and ungodly, to receive Christ crucified, dead and buried, and risen again; who is made a prince and a Saviour for such sinners as through the gospel shall be brought to believe on Him.

Augustus Toplady, the famous hymn-writer of the eighteenth century, admirably expresses the truth of the sinner's emptiness and the manner in which he needs to apply for mercy. As we come to Christ for mercy, and by him to our heavenly Father for salvation, we know that our guilt is the only qualification we have:

> Nothing in my hand I bring,
> Simply to thy cross I cling;
> Naked, come to thee for dress;
> Helpless, look to thee for grace;
> Foul, I to the fountain fly;
> Wash me, Saviour, or I die!

9.
The primacy of preaching

Many pressures, as I intend to show, are at work today to downgrade preaching and relegate it to a subservient place in the life of the church.

In the face of such pressures we can be inspired by the example of the Puritans, who maintained the primacy of preaching. Important principles, or axioms, undergirded their view of preaching and my purpose here is to examine these. In this way we shall see why we should maintain preaching as the high point of the worship service and the primary means of conversion and of building up and edifying God's people.

Underlying the preaching of the Puritans are three basic axioms:[1]

1. The unique place of preaching is to convert, feed and sustain.
2. The life of the preacher must radiate the reality of what he preaches.
3. Prayer and solid Bible study are basic to effective preaching.

1. The unique place of preaching is to convert, feed and sustain

Arthur Hildersam sums up this principle when he asserts: 'Preaching was the chief work of all that Christ, the chief pastor, was sent to do in his ministry (Luke 4:18,43) — neither was there any one work of his calling that he did so much and so diligently exercise himself in as in preaching. Christ sent me, saith the apostle (1 Corinthians 1:17), not to baptize (that is not so much to baptize) but to preach the gospel — and this is the chief work that we are called of God to exercise ourselves in — gladly taking all opportunities for doing this work.'[2]

The Puritans studied hard in order to be exemplary preachers. They maintained that this was their primary calling and they laboured to maintain the primacy of preaching. No other means of grace addresses the whole person — mind, affections, conscience and will — like powerful preaching. Nothing else is used by God the Holy Spirit in the unique way that preaching is. The Son of Man himself came to preach, as did John the Baptist who prepared the way for him. The multitude did not go out into the wilderness to hear a classroom lecture from John the Baptist. A rock formed his pulpit and the heavens his sounding-board. He preached in such a fashion that multitudes were prepared to walk many miles to hear him. And when these hearers arrived John did not flatter them, or set out to make them feel good. He aimed straight at their consciences and addressed them as the needy, lost sinners that they were.

Tremendous forces conspire to deny preaching the primary place today. In America especially, there is a tendency to displace preaching with entertainment in the form of song and musical items, so that preaching is just tagged on at the end. In some charismatic churches the Bible hardly features at all, let alone expository preaching. Healings and signs and sensational testimonies form the main attractions. This reminds us of Paul's saying that the 'Jews demand miraculous signs,' to which the apostle's response was: 'But we preach Christ crucified.'

The primacy of preaching in the preacher's own life is often usurped by programmes. His energies are sapped and his time consumed by administrative duties. These deprive him of an effective preaching ministry. In this matter it is necessary to avoid the extreme illustrated by the description of the preacher said to be invisible for six days of the week and incomprehensible on the seventh! A balance is to be kept. Pastoring and caring for people are vital, but the imperative exercise of study must not be neglected. The Scriptures liken the expositor to an ox treading out the grain (1 Tim. 5:18). Don Carson of Trinity College, Deerfield, maintains that he does not know of one effective expository Bible preacher in the USA who has not taken rigorous measures to protect the primacy of prayer and study (Acts 6:4). There are mega-congregations in the USA which have been built up through expository preaching.

Sometimes Christians have a distorted view of how the Holy Spirit works. I heard of a pastor who announced that from now on he was going to get his sermons directly from heaven! He abandoned the work of the study. Immediately his ministry became repetitive and shallow and after six months of starvation the church officers asked him to leave. It is misguided to imagine that the Holy Spirit directly communicates and inspires preaching and that it is therefore unspiritual to write out sermons or to follow carefully prepared outlines. The Holy Spirit honours prayerful, dedicated work: 'Do your best to present yourself to God as one approved, a workman who does not need to be ashamed and who correctly handles the word of truth' (2 Tim. 2:15).

Effective expository preaching requires enormous discipline of mind and heart. When the preacher decides on a series of expositions this is a major undertaking which should be arrived at only after fervent prayer and meditation. When a series is begun the preacher is wise to keep his options open. If he and the congregation find that they do not experience the blessing of the Holy Spirit, it may be appropriate to take another direction from the one originally planned, for the Scripture is an inexhaustible source of truth and edification.

A further subtle undermining of the primacy of preaching is by the concept that discussion groups serve the interests of Christ's kingdom better than preaching. Occasional discussion groups can be useful to debate relevant issues, especially congregational concerns or practical matters which affect the life of the church or the community. But when it comes to knowing and applying the Bible, discussion groups must rate a third-best. Each person brings an 'itsy bit' — a good thought here and a little word there. That is a poor substitute for preaching. When the preacher brings the Word to bear in its context and applies it with spiritual power to the congregation they are lifted up, encouraged by the sense of God's presence and motivated and renewed in a way that is unlikely in a discussion group.

2. The life of the preacher must radiate the reality of what he preaches

Prominent in the minds of hearers, especially visitors, as they listen to a preacher is the question: 'Does this man live out what he preaches?' Moses' companions had no doubt about whose company Moses had kept when he came down from Mount Sinai. Paul exhorted Timothy: 'Watch your life and doctrine closely. Persevere in them, because if you do, you will save both yourself and your hearers' (1 Tim. 4:16).

Addressing ministers, Richard Baxter wrote, 'Content not yourselves with being in a state of grace, but be also careful that your graces are kept in vigorous and lively exercise, and that you preach to yourselves the sermons which you study, before you preach them to others.'

The apostle Paul was able to commend his way of life to Timothy: 'You, however, know all about my teaching, my way of life, my purpose, faith, patience, love, endurance, persecutions, sufferings' (2 Tim. 3:10).

The close connection between the holy life of the preacher and the flock to which he preaches is apparent in a further statement from Baxter: 'If we let our love decline, we are not likely to raise up theirs. If we feed on unwholesome food, either errors or fruitless controversies, our hearers are like to fare the worse for it. Whereas, if we abound in faith, and love, and zeal, how would it overflow to the refreshing of our congregations, and how would it appear in the increase of the same graces in them!'

If hypocrisy is to be avoided then the preacher needs to epitomize in his own lifestyle and in his demeanour the message that he is preaching.

3. Prayer and solid Bible study are basic to effective preaching

It was while facing conflict and criticism that the apostles asserted that their priorities were prayer and study: 'It would not be right for us to neglect the ministry of the word of God in order to wait on tables. Brothers, choose seven men from among you who are known to be full of the Spirit and wisdom. We will turn this responsibility over to them and will give our attention to prayer and the ministry of the word' (Acts 6:2-4).

What minister is not the object of criticism, some of it warranted? We cannot please everyone, but must seek to please the Lord in everything. How do we answer criticisms? Our answer is prayer. We are not above contradiction; indeed we should encourage our hearers to share their criticisms with us. With some we can use humour about ourselves so they may see that we genuinely seek to strive after humility. But spiritual attitudes can only be maintained through a life of prayer.

As a race of ministers the Puritans excelled in holding to the prime place of preaching, but they did so in a balanced way. They did not neglect their role as physicians of the soul with a responsibility to counsel and encourage personally the members of the church. We live in very different times with a different set of pressures; nevertheless we can derive inspiration from their example.

For instance, at a little village in Somerset called Mells was a minister, Richard Fairclough. When he died in 1682 aged sixty-one, John Howe preached his funeral sermon in which he tells us how that people from miles around used to throng to hear Fairclough preach: 'O how that congregation hath been wont to melt under his most fruitful ministry. His prayers, sermons, and other ministerial performances had that strange pungency, quickness and authority with them, at some times; that softness, gentleness, sweetness, alluringness at others, that one would think it scarcely possible to resist the spirit and power by which he spoke. And the effect did in blessed measure correspond; they became a much enlightened, knowing, judicious, reformed, religious people. His labours were almost incredible. His whole heart was in his work. Every day, for many years together, he used to rise at three in the morning, or sooner, and to be with God (which was his dear delight) when others slept.'[3]

This example illustrates the point that the Puritans succeeded in their ministries because they excelled in the basics. We today can do as well as they did if we maintain a balance in the work of prayer and preaching together with the care of souls. With regard to the principle of basics there is the analogy of music or sport. A musician will never excel unless he is proficient and disciplined in basic skills. Expression in rendering pieces can only follow expertise in basic skills. The same is true in sports. A player will never excel at a game like golf unless he masters the basics. In the ministry a man is called to be spiritual. He must excel in godliness and holiness of life. That is basic. Then he must work in prayer and intercession and at the same time discipline his mind incessantly in study and meditation as he prepares for the pulpit. He must think about his calling and apply himself to it constantly.

Prayer embraces the people to whom we minister. 'Far be it from me that I should sin against the LORD by failing to pray for you' (1 Sam. 12:23). We relate to the lives and needs of the people we address in preaching.

The Puritans did not neglect their role as physicians of the soul with a responsibility to counsel and encourage personally the members of the church.

10.
Imaginative expository preaching

The practice of systematic expository preaching has become much more widespread in recent years. Dr Martyn Lloyd-Jones is regarded by many as the foremost preacher in the British Isles during the twentieth century. He followed the systematic expository method and in so doing inspired a whole generation of preachers to follow that method, a way which was exemplified by the Puritans.

Spurgeon did not use the systematic procedure of preaching through books or sections of Scripture. He explained that he needed freedom as week by week he was confronted with the huge challenge to be an evangelist. At every meeting thousands gathered to hear him, many being visitors from other places or from other countries. The Tabernacle was filled twice on Sunday and then again at a preaching service on Thursday evening. Although he loved the Puritans, in this particular matter Spurgeon felt the necessity of complete freedom to take a different text every time he preached. In preaching a series of sermons it is necessary to recap, but of course Spurgeon could proceed straight to his subject.

For the great majority of preachers, however, the systematic method is best. The essential ingredients of powerful effective preaching can be summarized as follows:

1. Expository
2. Progressional or systematic
3. Exegetical
4. Doctrinal (instructional)
5. Structural

6. Applicatory (pastoral)
7. Practical
8. Experimental
9. Trinitarian
10. Evangelistic
11. Powerful (spiritually compelling)
12. Popular (relevant and attractive)

These characteristics can be used like a check-list. When a preacher is coming near to completing the preparation of his sermon, he may well ask the following questions: Is this sermon really expository? Is my text in harmony with the context? Is it exegetical? Have I fathomed the precise meaning of the text, or am I making it say what I would like it to say? Is there doctrinal instruction? Will my hearers be built up in the great central truths of the faith? Have I assembled my material with the best possible structure? In other words, is it easy to follow, logically connected and easy to remember? As I preach this sermon am I dealing with my people pastorally? Am I mindful of, and sympathetic with, their struggles and temptations? And is this exposition practical? What are they expected to do about it? Is my sermon experimental? Will hearts be warmed? Will Christians be delighted in their union with Father, Son and Holy Spirit?

And what about those in the congregation who do not believe? How will this affect them? Will it be powerful? How can I bring my hearers to repentance towards God and faith in our Lord Jesus Christ? Will I be used to compel them to come in? (Luke 14:23). What is there about my sermon which makes it appealing and attractive? Our Lord used references to nature and Thomas Watson used delightful pithy metaphors and similes. How can I emulate my Master and some of his best servants to make my preaching the effective vehicle of salvation and edifying to believers?

It is difficult, if not impossible, to do justice to all these requirements all the time. It is a mistake to pack too much into one sermon. The average person is limited in the amount of material he can absorb in one sitting. The best kind of preaching, rarely achieved, is the kind in which one principal point is driven home in such a way that the hearers never forget the impact.

The task is exceedingly difficult. Paul says, 'And who is equal to such a task?' (2 Cor. 2:16). Although John Bunyan was the most underprivileged of the Puritans from the point of view of a formal university education, he came closest to exemplifying all the features outlined above. Bunyan can be an encouragement to many who feel inferior because they have lacked the advantages of seminary training.

The Puritans are especially helpful when it comes to structure in expository preaching. They developed a knack of drawing out the meaning of the text and applying its teaching to their hearers. Some examples will illustrate this.

For instance, take John Flavel on 'Come unto me, all ye that labour and are heavy laden, and I will give you rest' (Matt. 11:28, AV). Flavel divides up his text as follows:

Three things are especially remarkable:

1. The soul's distress, 'weary and heavy laden';
2. The invitation to come to Christ under that burden, 'Come to me';
3. The encouragement from Christ, 'I will give you rest.'

A further example is taken from Stephen Charnock on the text, 'A bruised reed shall he not break, and a smoking flax shall he not quench, till he send forth judgement unto victory' (Matt. 12:20, AV).

1. *First* the subject, 'A bruised reed and a smoking flax'.
2. *Second* the act, 'He will not break and he will not quench'.
3. *Third* the continuance of it, 'Till he sends forth judgement to victory'.

Richard Sibbes, expounding this same text, makes his application in this way:

Doctrinal — grace is little at firsthand; Christ will not quench small and weak beginnings;
Practical — tenderness is required in ministers towards young beginners;
Experimental — Christ is a physician expert in treating all diseases, especially the binding of a broken heart.

Thomas Brooks commences his *Precious Remedies against Satan's Devices* with an exposition of 2 Corinthians 2:11: 'Lest Satan should get an advantage of us: for we are not ignorant of his devices' (AV). Setting the text in context Brooks then proceeds:

1. To prove that Satan uses devices.
2. To show what these devices are; and
3. To expound the remedies against Satan's devices.

In this way Brooks lays a foundation for a short series on the subject.

Scripture varies a great deal in character. There is history, doctrine (e.g. Romans and Ephesians), narrative, wisdom literature, the parables of our Lord, apocalyptic writing (e.g. Daniel chapters 7-12 and Revelation chapters 4-22). The diverse nature of Scripture demands great versatility in expository methods. The expositor must pray for freedom and flexibility in setting out the salient points and in extracting and applying the main truths intended.

For consistent structured and balanced outlines that draw out the meaning and message of the text Thomas Manton is to be recommended.

It is evident that after preaching the Puritans selected much of their material for further development and publication. In this way we have preserved to us the legacy of Puritan literature, almost all of which originated in their preaching.

On the subject of writing, Francis Bacon (1561-1626) declared, 'Reading maketh a full man, conference a ready man and writing an exact man.' While it may not be practicable to write out every sermon in full, it is important for the expositor to construct the framework and then write out any sections in which there may be weakness, obscurity, or lack of clarity. Calvin's commentaries are still sought after and highly valued today because he is noted for explaining the principal points with maximum lucidity. He exemplifies Bacon's 'exact man'. We cannot edify when we are obscure.

In our day special skill is needed to arouse interest and keep attention. Those of us who are called to preach will do better at it if we follow the Puritan method of using arresting headings and structures which are true to the text but handled in an imaginative and versatile way. A vital part of expository preaching is the use of illustrations which fit the subject in hand. If we can draw our illustrative material from the Scriptures all the better. The Puritans varied in the amount of illustration they used but they excelled in drawing their material from the Scriptures. However, illustrations can also be taken from current events to drive home the relevance of the gospel message.

Note the effect produced by the best preacher of all, our Lord himself. When the chief priests sent temple guards to arrest Jesus they were helpless to carry out the command and testified: 'No one ever spoke the way this man does'(John 7:46). It will be a great day when preaching is revived as God's instrument to convict the world of guilt, righteousness and judgement. We can be sure that it will be imaginative preaching which arrests the hearts and minds of the hearers.

'Reading maketh a full man, conference a ready man and writing an exact man' (Francis Bacon).

11.
The reality of sin

The Puritans were strongest where we are weakest today. This is especially true with regard to the doctrine of sin.

There are a number of important factors which underline the urgent need to be clear about what sin is. The principal ones are set out in the following paragraphs.

Firstly, we live in the climate of postmodernism. Western society encourages sin to an enormous extent and resists definition of, or clarity about, sin. Postmodernist philosophy is fiercely antinomian, that is, opposed to law. Right and wrong are judged on the basis of subjective human feelings. The result is a slide into an abyss of lawlessness. The consequences of lawlessness are seen in the alarming increase in family break-up, divorce, crime and overcrowded prisons. An example of a book which deals with this theme is *The Vanishing Conscience* by John F. MacArthur Jr, a study which demonstrates that failure to deal with sin as sin lies at the foundation of America's moral collapse.[1]

Secondly, a ministry which is weak and flabby on the subject of sin is a useless ministry. A preaching ministry that does not result in conviction of sin is useless. If it does not wound, how can it heal? The good news is only for sinners. The unbelieving world caricatures and mocks preachers. They are sometimes depicted as silly, soft and effeminate. At other times the typical preacher is portrayed as one who bellows and raves. The young Spurgeon was by far the most effective preacher of his time but was fiercely ridiculed and opposed in the press. Those who are truly called know that the Word of God is as sharp as a two-edged sword and that their business is to wield that sword (Heb. 4:12).

Thirdly, 'Christ and him crucified' is our theme (1 Cor. 2:2). Christianity is unique as it alone deals faithfully with the root problem of mankind, which is sin. And Christianity is also unique in that it provides the only effectual remedy for sin. Christ appeared that he might take away our sins. He who knew no sin was made to be sin for us that we might become the righteousness of God in him (2 Cor. 5:21). The enormity of sin is seen in the death of deaths that was Christ's. Millions of dollars are invested in scientific laboratories to seek solutions for disease, but our business, as pastors and preachers, is to deal clearly and faithfully with sin, its nature, guilt and consequences, and then to present the remedy which is found uniquely and only in the blood and sacrifice of Christ. 'Behold, the Lamb of God who takes away the sin of the world!' (John 1:29, NKJV).

Fourthly, without a biblical understanding of sin we cannot deal correctly and faithfully with the great central themes of life, namely, creation and the historic space-time fall of Adam and Eve, the nature of law, the place of conscience, the history of redemption, Christ's active and passive work, regeneration, sanctification, ultimate judgement and eternal heaven and hell.

Fifthly, arising out of the above, no reality is more terrible in all the universe than eternal hell. Sin is the principal explanation for why there should be such a thing.

The Puritans were direct in their treatment of this subject in a variety of treatises. They dealt comprehensively with the topic of sin. Jeremiah Burroughs, in his book *The Evil* of *Evils*,[2] declared of sin that it makes a man conformable to the devil, 'for sin is of the same nature as the devil and a furtherance of the devil's kingdom in the world'.

The strengths of Puritan teaching may be summarized under four headings: first, they used God's moral law to define sin; secondly, they expounded the truth of original sin; thirdly, they stressed the necessity of mortification of sin and, fourthly, they warned of eternal punishment.

1. The Puritans used God's moral law to define sin

Ralph Venning (1621-1674), a popular preacher in London four years after bubonic plague swept the city in 1665, wrote a book which he called *The Plague of Plagues*,[3] an apt title since there is no plague like the plague of sin, which kills every member of the human race. Physical death is the first death. The plague of sin is also responsible for the second death, whereby all those who die in their sins are subject to eternal punishment in hell. Venning divides his exposition into four parts: first, what sin is; second, the sinfulness of sin; third, the witnesses against sin; and, fourth, application, in which he describes the good news of how to escape from the guilt and power of sin. Venning begins his treatise with a definition:

> Sin is the transgression of a law, yea of a good law, yea of God's law. Sin presupposes that there is a law in being, for where there is no law there is no transgression (Rom. 4:15). But where there is sin, there is a law, and a transgression of the law. Whosoever commits sin transgresses also the law, for sin is a transgression of the law (1 John 3:4). That this is the sin intended in our text is apparent from Romans 7:7. Now the law not only forbids the doing of evil, whether by thought, word or deed, but also commends the doing of good. So to omit the good

> command is sin, as well (or ill) as is the doing of the evil that is forbidden.

Edward Reynolds (1593-1676) was an eminent preacher greatly skilled in the Greek language. He served in the Westminster Assembly and wrote a treatise entitled *The Sinfulness of Sin*. This principally consists of an exposition of Romans 7:9: 'Once I was alive apart from law; but when the commandment came, sin sprang to life and I died.' Reynolds shows that a man may have the letter of the law and yet be without it in power and spirit. But the Holy Spirit takes the law and convinces a man that he is in a state of sin. He continues:

> Now the law gives life and strength to sin in three ways: First, by way of the curse and obligation of it, binding the soul with the guilt of sin to the judgement of the great day. Second, by the irritation of the law: 'Sin took occasion by the law, and so by the commandment became exceeding sinful.' Third, by conviction, laying open the wideness of sin to the conscience. As a serpent seems dead in the snow but is revived by heat, so sin seems dead when covered by ignorance but when awakened a man finds himself in the mouth of death.[4]

The majority of Puritans placed much stress on the preaching of the law to bring men to an awareness of sin. William Perkins knew that true repentance was the result of gospel grace, but he opposed those who for this reason would despise the preaching of the law. Anthony Burgess declared that the exhibition of 'the pure, strict and exact obligation of the Law' makes 'all thy deformities' to appear, and so 'in this sense it is good to be a legal preacher, and a legal hearer often'. He considered that this legal preaching was 'the great work that the ministers of God have to do in their congregations in these times. Men must come to the knowledge of sin in themselves, by the Law', and this is no 'easy matter', but 'It is the preaching of the Law of God ... that will ... discover to them their hidden and secret sins; never was any brought to a sight of his sins ... but only by the preaching of the Law of God.'[5]

2. The Puritans expounded the truth of original sin

Thomas Goodwin, in his great work *An Unregenerate Man's Guiltiness Before God in Respect of Sin and Punishment,* proceeds directly to the root of the matter, namely, original sin.[6] He begins with Romans 5:12: 'Wherefore, as by one man sin entered into the world, and death by sin; and so death passed upon all men, for that all have sinned' (AV). Goodwin shows from Romans chapters 1-3 that sin has universally overtaken the world, not one person excepted. Having established the truth of original sin and guilt, Goodwin proceeds to show how corruption has overtaken man in all his faculties, his understanding, affections, conscience and will.

The Puritan doctrine of original sin is expounded, among others, by David Clarkson, Thomas Watson, John Flavel, John Owen, and later in the same tradition by Thomas Boston and Jonathan Edwards.[7] The clearest definition which sums up the doctrine of original sin is that of the *Larger Westminster Catechism*:

> *Question:* Wherein consists the sinfulness of that estate into which man fell?
>
> *Answer:* The sinfulness of that estate whereinto man fell consists in the guilt of Adam's first sin, the loss of that righteousness in which he was created, and the corruption of his nature, whereby he is utterly indisposed, disabled, and made opposite to all that is spiritually good, and wholly inclined to all evil, and that continually; which is commonly called original sin, and from which all actual transgressions proceed.

Similar wording is found in chapter 6 of the *Westminster Confession*, paragraph 4. In a modern English version of the *1689 Baptist Confession* the corresponding paragraph reads:

> The actual sins that men commit are the fruit of the corrupt nature transmitted to them by our first parents. By reason of this corruption, all men become wholly inclined to all evil; sin disables them. They are utterly indisposed to, and, indeed, rendered opposite to, all that is good.[8]

All born to Adam inherit[9] his guilt and corruption. The clause 'rendered opposite to all that is good' does not mean that every person is as bad as he possibly could be. There is an enormous amount of good in the world. This good we ascribe to the loving-kindness of God. We call it common grace. God's common grace is widely misconstrued since it is argued that since there is so much good in the world, this gloomy view of sin which I have been describing cannot be correct. But it is correct. Man's depravity is stark. Recall the two great World Wars of the twentieth century, the holocaust organized by the Nazis (six million Jews perished in the extermination camps plus a further six million who were classed as belonging to undesirable categories), and the Gulag (eighteen million perished in the death camps in the Soviet Union under Stalin). The genocide in Cambodia, Rwanda/Burundi, Yugoslavia and, at the time of writing, the murders in East Timor all bear gruesome witness to the depravity of man. World history is a saga of sin and suffering but life would be intolerable were it not for the tremendous power exercised by the Holy Spirit to restrain sin and keep it under control.

It can be argued, if man is fallen in all his faculties, why expend effort to persuade him to believe and repent? The answer is that the Holy Spirit uses preaching and literature to invade the dominions of darkness. He is the Spirit of regeneration. He uses the proclamation of biblical truth to arrest and convert. He convinces the world of sin, righteousness and judgement to come (John 16:8).

Adam was given a specific law. He represented the whole human race. Through his act in breaking that law his guilt is imputed to all his descendants. Thomas Watson suggests that much was involved in that first sin, including unbelief, ingratitude, discontent, pride, disobedience, theft, presumption, carelessness (lack of thought or consideration) and murder.[10] Murder is involved because Adam had been told most clearly that in the day he ate that fruit he would die. In his sin, therefore, he murdered his posterity. Watson places unbelief at the head of his list.

Stephen Charnock, in an exposition of John 16:9, 'Of sin, because they believe not on me' (AV), also asserts that unbelief is the fountain of all sins and suggests that God has to employ the highest means to bring men to a sense of the sin of unbelief.[11] Of all sins unbelief is the most harmful because it is a sin against the only remedy available.

Adam stood in the place of us all in his disobedience and sin. What he did was in effect what all his posterity, each and every one of us, did. Thomas Manton expresses it this way: 'We saw the forbidden fruit with his eyes, gathered it with his hands, ate it with his mouth; that is, we were ruined by those things as though we had been there and consented to his acts.'[12]

Original sin is not an easy truth to grasp. Herman Bavinck, the great Dutch theologian, declares that this question is the second greatest enigma that exists. The origin of being is the first enigma. Bavinck adds that the origin of sin is certainly the hardest cross for man's understanding to bear.[13]

3. The Puritans stressed the necessity of mortification of sin

John Owen's exposition on the mortification of sin in believers is a classic work. In it he expounds Romans 8:13 under the following heads:

1. A duty prescribed: 'mortify the deeds of the body';
2. The persons denoted: 'you', 'if *you* mortify...';
3. The promise attached: 'you shall live';
4. The means employed: 'if you *through the Spirit*';
5. The condition: '*if* you mortify'.[14]

Owen stresses that the Christian should all his life make it his business to mortify the power of indwelling sin. 'The vigour, and power, and comfort of our spiritual life depends on the mortification of the deeds of the flesh.' He warns sternly of the power that lies in unmortified sin:

> Sin aims always at the utmost; every time it rises up to tempt or entice, if it has its own way, it will go out to the utmost sin in that kind. Every unclean thought or glance would be adultery if it could, every thought of unbelief would be atheism if allowed to develop. Every rise of lust, if it has its way, reaches the height of villainy; it is like the grave that is never satisfied. The deceitfulness of sin is seen in that it is modest in its first proposals but when it prevails it hardens men's hearts, and brings them to ruin.

Owen quotes Hebrews 3:13 which tells us that sin deceives — 'the deceitfulness of sin'. Remember how sin deceived the Israelites in the wilderness when they hardened their hearts.

Thomas Manton, in an exposition of Romans 6:14, 'For sin shall not have dominion over you; for ye are not under the law, but under grace' (AV), reasons that:

> There is still sin in us, a bosom enemy which is born and bred with us, and therefore soon will get the advantage of grace, if it be not well watched and resisted, as nettles and weeds, which are kindly to the soil, and grow of their own accord, will soon choke flowers, which are planted by care and industry, when they are neglected and not continually rooted out. We cannot get rid of this cursed inmate till this outward tabernacle be dissolved, and this house of clay be crumbled into dust, like ivy gotten into a wall, that will not be destroyed till the wall be pulled down.[15]

Mortification of sin extends to thoughts of the mind. Obadiah Sedgwick explains the words, 'Cleanse me from secret sins' (Ps. 19:12, AV), in the following way: 'Secret sins will become public sins if they are not cleansed. If you suppress them not in their root, you shall shortly see them break out in the fruit. A fire catches first the inside of the house and if not put out makes its way to the outside: "Lust when it has conceived brings forth sin" (James 1:15).'[16]

Sometimes we are deeply shocked by the falling into sin followed by the complete apostasy of those who have been highly esteemed as preachers and leaders in the church. This is a reminder that no believer is exempt from the necessity of mortifying sin. Often there is very real pain involved in mortification. Jeremiah Burroughs' principal thrust in his great book *The Evil of Evils* is that there is more evil in the smallest sin than in the greatest affliction. He points out that the heroes described in Hebrews chapter 11 chose and preferred to suffer the most terrible afflictions rather than to sin by denying their faith.

4. The Puritans warned of eternal punishment

Ralph Venning describes the hell into which Jesus descended in the bearing away of our sins: 'He suffered all kinds of sufferings. He suffered in every part and member of his body from head to foot. He suffered in his soul. He cried out on the cross, "My God, my God, why have you forsaken me?" He had all kinds of aggravating circumstances united in his sufferings.' 'The greatness of Christ's sufferings is a full witness against the sinfulness of sin.'[17]

Christ's achievement to atone for and take away our sin is immense. This is appreciated when we see what every sin deserves. Venning does not shrink from telling of the appalling torments which result from sin: 'Hell is the centre of all punishments, sorrow and pain, wrath and vengeance, fire and darkness...' 'These torments will be without intermission and will be for ever ... there will be aggravations of these torments for those who have lived long in sin, those who have had more opportunity to repent, and more knowledge, and for apostates who have turned their backs on God.'[18]

Ralph Venning displays a wonderful ability to have the text of Scripture exercise its own power. He proceeds:

> The persons sentenced: 'those on his left hand'.
> The sentence: 'Depart from me'.
> The state they are in: 'cursed'.
> The torment: 'everlasting fire'.
> The company that is theirs: 'the devil and his angels'.[19]

The weight of the guilt of sin is stressed by John Flavel in his treatise on the soul of man: 'The guilt of all sin gathers to, and settles in the conscience of every Christless sinner, and makes up a vast treasure of guilt in the course of his life in this world.'[20]

George Swinnock (1627-1673), in a deeply moving exposition on Matthew 25:41 entitled 'The sinners' last sentence', exposes the guilt of law-breakers: 'He breaks the whole law by breach of any one of them, because he sins against love, and breaks that bond and knot which keeps and fastens the whole law together.'[21]

In a sermon on the same text Richard Adams concludes by reminding his hearers that our Lord urged that we are to fear him who is able to destroy both soul and body in hell (Luke 12:5). Adams exhorts to flee speedily from sin by repentance and holds up the superlative love of Christ displayed in undergoing the punishment that was our due. 'O let us now bathe our souls in the blood of Christ that everlasting burnings may not hereafter seize upon us.'[22]

Without a biblical understanding of sin we cannot deal correctly and faithfully with the great central themes of life.

Appendix I
Were the Puritans narrow-minded bigots?

To most people today the Puritans were a narrow-minded, bigoted body of people who dressed in black and hated fun. This is a popular caricature. A scholarly volume has been written which examines carefully what the Puritans were really like. Leland Ryken's book *Worldly Saints — The Puritans as they Really Were*[1] corrects ill-informed views of the Puritans. Ryken's book draws from both the English Puritans and the Puritans who settled in America and came to be known as the New England Puritans, whereas I confine this book to the English Puritans. It is true that the New England Puritans developed their own character. Nevertheless Ryken's observations help us gain a balanced picture of Puritan character on both sides of the Atlantic.

In very abbreviated form Ryken's assessments look like this:

- *The Puritans were against sex.* Ridiculous.
- *The Puritans never laughed and were opposed to fun.* Only partly true. The Puritans were serious people, but they also said such things as this: 'God would have our joys to be far more than our sorrows.'
- *The Puritans wore drab, unfashionable clothes.* Untrue. The Puritans dressed according to the fashion of their class and time.
- *The Puritans were opposed to sports and recreation.* Largely false. A book-length study has shown that the Puritans enjoyed such varied activities as hunting, fishing, a form of football, bowling, reading, music, swimming, skating and archery.

- *The Puritans were money-grabbing workaholics who would do anything to get rich.* Generally untrue. The Puritans were in fact obsessed with the *dangers* of wealth.
- *The Puritans were hostile to the arts.* Partly true, but not as true as most people today think. The misunderstanding stems from the fact that the Puritans removed music and art from the churches. But this was an objection to Roman Catholic forms of worship and ceremony, not to music and art in themselves.
- *The Puritans were over-emotional and denigrated reason.* Nonsense. They aimed at a balance of head and heart.
- *Puritanism was an old-fashioned movement that appealed only to people over seventy suffering from tired blood.* Absolutely wrong. Puritanism was a youthful, vigorous movement. C. S. Lewis calls the early Puritans, 'young, fierce, progressive intellectuals, very fashionable and up-to-date'.
- *The Puritans were repelled by the human body and the physical world.* Not true.
- *The Puritans were intolerant towards people who disagreed with them.* True by modern standards, but not by the standards of their day. *No* group in the sixteenth and seventeenth centuries was prepared to grant full religious and political toleration.
- *The Puritans were overly strict.* Often true. Samuel Ward's college diary consists of a cataloguing of his failings, and his self-accusations include such offences as these: going 'to bed without prayer', falling asleep without his last thought being about God, 'unwillingness to pray'.
- *The Puritans repressed normal human feelings in the name of religion.* Not at all. The Puritans were warmly human in their feelings.
- *The Puritans were legalistic moralists who judged people by their external behaviour only.* Largely untrue of the original Puritans.
- *The Puritans indulged in too much self-loathing.* Partly true. Cotton Mather wrote this type of thing in his diary: 'A Christian ought always to think humbly of himself, and be full of self-abasing reflections. By loathing of himself continually, and being very sensible of what are his

own loathsome circumstances, a Christian does what is very pleasing to Heaven.'

- *The Puritans were ignorant people who opposed education.* Absolutely untrue. No Christian movement in history has been more zealous for education.

Appendix II
How do Baptists relate to the Puritans?

We have seen that John Bunyan was an exemplar of Puritanism in preaching, in life-style and in writing. As has been pointed out earlier, he was not strictly speaking a Puritan in the sense of his church affiliation because of his nonconformity. For his unwillingness to compromise he suffered twelve years' imprisonment.

Baptists grew out of Puritanism and multiplied, especially during the 1640s and 1650s. We have seen this in the lives of Hanserd Knollys and Henry Jessey. A detailed account of the emergence of the Baptists from the Puritan times is provided by Prof. Michael Haykin in his book *Kiffin, Knollys and Keach.*[1] In scintillating fashion Prof. Haykin describes the lives of 'the three Ks'. A brief look at one of these will give an idea of the story.

Hanserd Knollys (1599-1691) studied for the ministry at Catherine Hall, Cambridge, and entered the ministry in Lincolnshire. However, in 1635 his Puritan convictions led him to make a complete break with the Church of England. He left for America in the same year but returned in 1641. He worked with the Baptists and became one of their outstanding leaders, being one of those who signed the *1646 Baptist Confession of Faith*. Knollys pastored a large Baptist church in London which was attended by a congregation of about a thousand.

An account of the developments preceding the formulation of the *1677 London Baptist Confession of Faith* is provided in the book *Our Baptist Heritage.*[2] When conditions improved in 1688 it was possible to publish the Confession which had been formulated earlier but persecution made it inexpedient to circulate the work widely. The 1677 Confession became known as *The 1689 Confession of Faith* only because of its wider publicity at that time. *The Westminster Confession* represents the doctrines of the Puritans. The Baptists based their Confession of Faith on the Puritan formulations as set out at Westminster, and the Congregational version of the Confession *(The Savoy Declaration).* Within the story of the Puritans it is fascinating to note that the leading non-Presbyterian divines involved in the *Savoy Declaration* were: John Owen, Thomas Goodwin, Philip Nye, William Bridge, Joseph Caryl, William Greenhill and John Howe. 120 churches were represented.

All three Puritan Confessions of Faith are the same in essence and differ only in terms of church government and baptism.

Persecution and the unfinished reformation

As we have observed, the story of the Puritans is one of constant persecution and harassment. In several ways this was worse after the restoration of the monarchy and the accession of Charles II. Appalling conditions of persecution continued right up to the time of the revolution in 1688. A brilliant book which covers the period from 1660 to 1689 is Michael Watts' *The Dissenters.*[3] This is scholarship at its best and at the same time provides gripping reading.

The persecution of the Puritans, the separatists and Baptists is simply a further miserable chapter in the history of that unholy alliance of church and state which began with Constantine in the fourth century. The church-state union virtually changed the face of Christianity for the next thousand years. The sixteenth-century Reformation was only partial. The Continental Baptists, dubbed Anabaptists, wished to go all the way and separate the church from the state. Zwingli and Luther could see that they could not succeed in the work of reformation without the support of the secular powers. From a pragmatic point of view they were right.

Christianity cannot be forced. Discipleship is essentially a voluntary matter. The story of the struggle between believers seeking freedom to maintain the biblical position of the church as a gathered body called out of the world, and secular or magisterial Christianity, is told by Leonerd Verduin in his books *The Reformers and their Stepchildren* and *The Anatomy of a Hybrid*. These books are classics which explain the history and the issues with wonderful lucidity.

From the time of King Henry VIII onwards we observe the granting of supreme power and authority over the Christian church in England to a monarch irrespective of his or her character or ability. It is easy to see how ludicrous that is when we read in 1 Timothy 3 that every elder and deacon in Christ's church should be of exemplary spiritual character. When the pope conferred upon Henry VIII the title 'The Defender of the Faith' the king could not restrain his delight, whereupon his court jester said to him, 'My good Harry, let me and thee defend each other, and let the faith alone to defend itself.' We see in the Puritan story a great deal of misery inflicted upon Christians in the interests of vested political power. It is the tradition in the Church of England that the monarch is the head of that church. At the time of writing Prince Charles is heir to the throne. If he becomes king he will automatically become head of the Church of England. He has stated that he is not interested in being defender of 'The Faith' but simply defender of 'Faith', thus showing that he does not understand the nature of evangelical biblical Christianity.

As Professors James McGoldrick[4] and Michael Haykin have shown, historical evidence is lacking to prove a connection between the Continental Anabaptists of the sixteenth century and the English Baptists. Yet both held firmly to the concept of the gathered nature of the church and that baptism is for believers only. Both held firmly to the separation of church and state. Both believed in liberty of conscience.

In his book *Kiffin Knollys and Keach* Haykin traces the emerging of two groups of Baptists in mid-seventeenth-century England. The Arminian or General Baptists formed a smaller group, while the Puritan or Calvinistic Baptists formed the major group which followed the Bunyan Puritan tradition. Baptists round the world today are rediscovering their roots and the richness of the legacies of Puritanism.

Appendix III
Oxford and Cambridge Universities

Readers will have observed that almost all the Puritans were educated at Oxford or Cambridge Universities. In present-day terms that sounds prestigious in the extreme since Cambridge and Oxford, in that order, top the table of excellence in a league table covering over one hundred British universities. Today to enter Oxford or Cambridge requires top examination grades plus passing special entry examinations, or else winning scholarships (of which there are a variety, both in Britain and overseas).

It may come as a surprise to some readers, but in England during the days of the Puritans there were no other choices. Oxford and Cambridge were the only universities. The academic standards and the discipline varied considerably and in the short sketch of the life of John Owen I referred to the difficulties he encountered as vice-chancellor in affecting much-needed reformation in the university. (Mostly the chancellor is a famous personality to give prestige to a university while the vice-chancellor is the person who has to do the actual work of administration.)

There is a fair amount of mythology about the emergence of Oxford and Cambridge Universities. This is cleared away by Alan B. Cobban in his book *The Medieval English Universities: Oxford and Cambridge.*[1] He shows that these institutions, like Paris and Bologna in France before them, gained university status gradually. Both Oxford and Cambridge became universities shortly after 1209. Before the emergence of universities, advanced education was provided at cathedral schools. The population of England in the fourteenth century could not easily justify a third university, especially when it is considered that both Oxford and Cambridge offered instruction in all four faculties — arts, law, theology and medicine.

Until the time of the Reformation the Universities of Oxford and Cambridge were under the jurisdiction of the Roman Catholic Church. The collegiate system developed which, apart from Durham University, is unique to Oxford and Cambridge. Each college is essentially independent while a central administration only collates matters of common interest. Colleges were originally founded and endowed by kings, queens, high-ranking statesmen or aristocrats.

There are about forty colleges at Oxford. I name a few with their dates of inception to give an idea of just how old — and how new — some of the colleges are: Balliol (1263), Merton (1264), Magdalen (1458), Wadham (1612), Pembroke (1624), Worcester (1714), Regent's Park (1810), Keble (1868) and Wolfston (1965).

The colleges at Cambridge number about twenty-four. These include Peterhouse (1284), Gonville and Caius (1384), King's (1441), Queen's (1448), Jesus (1496), Trinity (1546), Emmanuel (1584) and Sidney Sussex (1596) — the latter two having originally been endowed as Puritan colleges — Selwyn (1882) and Churchill (1960).

Some Scottish universities boast great antiquity: St Andrews (1411), Glasgow (1451), Aberdeen (1495), Edinburgh (1583).

After Oxford and Cambridge, London University is the oldest in England. It has the largest number of students — the most colleges, institutes and medical and dental schools. The University of Manchester was founded in 1851, and the Universities of Newcastle-on-Tyne in 1852, Birmingham 1900, Liverpool 1903, Leeds 1904, Sheffield 1905, Bristol 1909, Reading 1926, Nottingham 1948. Since then a university has been established in almost every major city of England.

Appendix IV
The Reformation in Scotland

In 1971 Dr Martyn Lloyd-Jones gave a paper at the Westminster Conference, London, with the title 'John Knox, The Founder of Puritanism'. That is correct as far as Scotland is concerned. The Reformation in Scotland has its own distinctive character and it is better for the sake of clarity to think in terms of two separate reformation movements. There are parallels, but the reformations in England and Scotland need to be traced out separately. Scotland became the land of Presbyterianism. That has never been the case in England. Today there are very few viable Presbyterian churches in England. Several hundred churches have adopted the London Baptist Confession of Faith, known as *The 1689 Baptist Confession of Faith,* as their doctrinal basis. Without these churches Puritanism would be almost extinct in England.

Scotland has a wonderful history of theological faithfulness to the Bible, a testimony which has enriched the wider church. When the churches in England declined during long periods in the seventeenth, eighteenth and nineteenth centuries there remained a solid core of Presbyterian orthodoxy in Scotland, a nation which also enjoys an outstanding history of revival. There is a lesson here. Fidelity to a confession is important. Whenever the Particular Baptists have wandered away from their Puritan heritage, as represented by *The 1689 Confession*, they have fallen into decline. When they have returned to those moorings they have revived and prospered.

While John Knox did exercise some influence in the progress of the Reformation in England, I suggest that it is appropriate that we should view him principally as a leader of the Reformation in Scotland. When we look to the antecedents in England, we rightly acclaim William Tyndale as the forerunner of Puritanism. Tyndale gave the common people of England the Bible. He was the first in a new line to defy the absolute power of the English monarch.

Characteristic of the Scottish Reformation was the manner in which the godly banded themselves together under the Lord by solemn oath for mutual assistance and support in the defence of the gospel and the advance of reformation. The earliest known bond or 'covenant' was made under the leadership of John Knox in 1556.

A National Covenant of about 1,000 words was written in 1580 which renounced Roman Catholicism root and branch. Alexander Henderson, a Reformed leader in Scotland in the 1630s, drew up 'The Solemn League and Covenant' in 1638. This covenant was approved at the General Assembly of Scotland in 1643 and again at a joint session of the English House of Commons and the Westminster Assembly. The subscribers swore to preserve the Reformed doctrine in Scotland and to aid reformation in England and Ireland and endeavour to remove all contrary systems, including Romanism, Episcopacy and heresy.

The Act of Uniformity which drove out over 2,000 ministers from their churches in 1662 in England also affected Scotland. Nearly 400, about a third of the ministers, were forced out of their churches. Draconian measures were taken against those who gathered in unauthorized meetings, called 'conventicles'. Fines, imprisonment, banishment and even slavery were suffered by those who continued to practise their faith according to their consciences. This period, known in England as the time of the Dissenters, was the time of the Covenanters in Scotland. The period 1685-1688 was especially cruel and became known as 'the killing time'. Many were put to death by soldiers without any recourse to law or to civil trial. Doctrinally the Covenanters held to the *Westminster Confession of Faith*. Many covenanting ministers were shot, hanged or sent into banishment until there were hardly any leaders left. The story is told by Alexander Smellie in *Men of the Covenant*.[1]

Appendix V
The Puritan / Westminster Conference

In 1950 a small study group began. It was known as the Puritan Conference and met in a room at the back of Westminster Chapel in London. By 1959 this annual meeting had grown into a two-day conference attended by 400. Dr James I. Packer and Dr D. Martyn Lloyd-Jones were the organizers. As materials on the Puritans became more easily accessible the attendance declined and for many years it has remained at around 220. Still meeting for two days at the same venue, it takes place in mid-December. Three papers are read each day followed by about an hour of discussion except for the closing session. There was no conference in 1970 and when the gathering convened again in 1971 the name was changed to the Westminster Conference. Since 1956 the papers have been published annually. The standard of research is generally high and in many cases outstanding. Ten papers originally given at the Puritan Conference by James Packer have appeared in his book *Among God's Giants* (see bibliography) and these are in the premier league as far as value and quality are concerned. Nineteen papers by Dr Martyn Lloyd-Jones given at the conference are gathered into a book with the title *The Puritans* and published by the Banner of Truth.

Some conference papers are biographies of Puritans: Thomas Goodwin by Brian Freer, Richard Sibbes by Maurice Roberts, Oliver Cromwell by Gordon Murray, Richard Baxter by Iain Murray, John Bunyan by Alan Gibson.

At the time of writing all the papers available total about 180. These provide an invaluable resource for those who love Puritanism. With the help of indices called 'The Finder' prepared by Michael Keen of Aberystwyth, subjects and authors can be located. This resource is increased in value as it is combined with all articles in the *Banner of Truth* magazine from its inception in 1955 and the bi-monthly journal *Reformation Today* from its inception in 1970. For instance, a researcher on John Owen will find thirteen references to Owen in the *Banner of Truth* magazine, six in *Reformation Today* and five in the *Puritan/Westminster Conference* papers.

Appendix VI
The ongoing influence of the Puritans

Whatever I write on the revival of Puritan literature today will be out of date very soon because the printing presses are constantly at work with new translations and newly edited and revised Puritan works. Readers who desire to read the Puritans should write and request catalogues from the major publishers of Puritan books.

A renewal of interest in the Puritans began in the late 1950s and accelerated in the 1960s. The Banner of Truth have led the way and published whole sets of Puritan writings: John Owen (16 vols plus 7 vols on Hebrews), John Flavel (6 vols), Thomas Brooks (6 vols), John Bunyan (3 large size vols), Stephen Charnock (5 vols), David Clarkson (3 vols), the beginning of the Thomas Manton set of 22 volumes, Richard Sibbes (7 vols) and George Swinnock (3 vols). Added to this are three volumes by Thomas Watson: *A Body of Divinity* (the first book published by the Banner and one of the most consistent sellers), *The Ten Commandments* and *The Lord's Prayer*. Also by Watson is *The Beatitudes*. A more recent Puritan title is George Newton on John 17 (394-page hardback). Newton was one of the ejected Puritans.

During 1997 the Banner of Truth published *A guide to the Puritans* by Robert P. Martin — a topical and textual index to the writings of the Puritans and some of their successors recently in print. This most useful tool enables students to locate biographies, sermons and meditations for the Lord's Table and sermons for special occasions.

The entire set of 22 volumes by Thomas Manton (1620-1677) was republished in 1870 with an introduction by J. C. Ryle in which he claimed that the Puritans did more to elevate the national character than any class of Englishmen that ever lived. During the 1970s an American publisher reissued the set of Thomas Manton, again in 22 volumes, an edition limited to 1,000. In 1996 another American publisher, Tanski Publications, has made available *The works of Thomas Goodwin* (1600-1680), in twelve volumes.

Added to this there are Banner of Truth popular paperback titles, some of the most useful of which are: *The Glory of Christ* and *Communion with God* and *Apostasy from the Gospel* by John Owen, *The Mystery of Providence* by John Flavel, *A Lifting up of the Downcast* by William Bridge, *Precious Remedies against Satan's Devices* by Thomas Brooks, *The Reformed Pastor* by Richard Baxter, *The True Bounds of Christian Freedom* by Samuel Bounds, *Heaven on Earth* by Thomas Brooks, *The Doctrine of Repentance* and *All Things for Good* both by Thomas Watson.

In the USA a publishing work of outstanding enterprise and energy has emerged, *Soli Deo Gloria.* Among the publications are the writings of Richard Baxter, (4 large vols), John Howe (3 vols), William Bridge (5 vols) and choice works by Jeremiah Burroughs including *The Excellency of a Gracious Spirit* and *The Evil of Evils*; Thomas Watson, including *Heaven Taken by Storm* and *The Duty of Self-Denial*; and Robert Bolton, including *A Treatise on Comforting Afflicted Consciences.* Edward Reynolds, who was one of the Westminster Assembly divines, wrote up his expositions on Psalm 110. This 465-page treasure is also available.

The influence of *The Westminster Confession of Faith* in Presbyterian denominations and of *The 1689 London Baptist Confession of Faith* is extensive. The 1689 Confession has been translated into a number of foreign languages.

The vision for abridging and simplifying some of the most useful Puritan writings has been implemented by Grace Baptist Mission. By 1999 there were sixteen titles (distributed by Evangelical Press). The idea of producing simplified Puritan classics originated through Tamil-speaking Christians in South India. John Owen's book *Death of Death* was chosen and renamed *Life by his Death.* The book was published in Tamil in 1981. One of the early fruits of this book was the conversion of a Tamil Hindu farmer in Sri Lanka. Four of Owen's titles are now printed in a variety of languages. For instance *The Glory of Christ* is available in Korean, Portuguese, Spanish and Tamil. Flavel's *Mystery of*

Providence is now in Hebrew, Spanish and Tamil, and Jeremiah Burroughs' *The Rare Jewel of Christian Contentment*, now entitled *Learning to be Happy*, is in Albanian, Arabic, French, Indonesian, Korean, Persian, Portuguese and Spanish. This catalogue of Puritan titles is growing steadily.

Notes

Foreword

1. *The Second London Confession of Faith* was formulated in 1677 and published when a new era of liberty dawned in 1689.

Introduction

1. Kent Philpott, *Are you really born again? — Understanding true and false conversion,* Evangelical Press, 1998 (144 pages).
2. John Flavel, *Christ Knocking at the Door of Sinners' Hearts,* Baker Book House, 400 pp.

Part I — The story of the Puritans

1. Robert Oliver, *The Recovery of the Reformed Faith in Twentieth Century England,* Evangelical Library Lecture for 1997. See also 'The Theological Renewal 1950-2000', *Reformation Today* No. 162.
2. Burroughs' classic is abridged and simplified with the title *Learning to be Happy* (Grace Publications, distributed by Evangelical Press).
3. J. R. Green, *Short History of the English People,* Macmillan, 1909 (first published 1878), p.460.
4. M. M. Knappen, *Tudor Puritanism,* Chicago Press, 1939, p.380.
5. John Spurr, *English Puritanism 1603-1689,* Macmillan,1998, pp.37,41.
6. Commended reading on the Great Ejection is Daniel Neal, *History of the Puritans,* Klock and Klock, 1979, vol. 3.
7. Kenneth Hylson-Smith, *The Churches in England from Elizabeth I to Elizabeth II, vol. 1, 1558-1688,* SCM, 1996, p.240, citing Loades, *The Mid-Tudor Crisis,* p.161.
8. Michael Watts, *The Dissenters — From the Reformation to the French Revolution,* Oxford University Press, 1985. Watts provides a detailed analysis of statistics
9. *Ibid.,* p.20, citing J. Stowe, *Three Fifteenth Century Chronicles,* ed. J. Gardiner (Camden Society, 1880, new series, xxviii. 143).
10. Hylson-Smith, *Churches in England,* p.61.
11. Patrick Collinson, *Godly People — Essays on English Protestantism and Puritanism,* Hambledon Press, 1983, p.1.
12. Spurr, *English Puritanism,* p.17.
13. Nicholas Tyacke, *Anti-Calvinist — The Rise of English Arminianism c.1590-1640,* Oxford, 1987, p.
14. Spurr, *English Puritanism,* p.171.

15. S. T. Bindoff, *Tudor England,* Pelican History of England, p.179.
16. Neal, *History of the Puritans,* vol. 1, p.124.
17. William Haller, *Foxe's Book of Martyrs and the Elect Nation,* Jonathan Cape, 1963, p.220ff.

Neville Williams, in a lecture published in 1975 by Dr Williams' Library, helpfully summarizes the development of Foxe's ever-increasing manuscript and its editions. The best edition of eight large volumes was edited by Josiah Pratt and published in 1853, a set of which can be found in the reference section of the Evangelical Library, London.

18. Haller, *Foxe's Book of Martyrs and the Elect Nation,* pp.224ff.
19. *Ibid.,* p.3.
20. I have drawn most of my material on the spiritual brotherhood from William Haller's, *The Rise of Puritanism,* Harper Torchbook, 1957, 464 pp., a most valuable resource which needs to be republished
21. Richard Rogers' 970-page exposition of Judges was republished in a facsimile edition by the Banner of Truth in 1983.
22. This title has been republished as a paperback by the Banner of Truth Trust.
23. Paul S. Seaver, *The Puritan Lectureships, The Politics of Religious Dissent, 1560-1662,* Stanford University Press, California, 1970, pp.172ff.
24. Spurr, *English Puritanism,* p.61.
25. Tyacke, *Anti-Calvinist,* pp.47ff.; cf. Spurr, *English Puritanism,* pp.81ff.
26. Spurr, *English Puritanism,* p.86.
27. Thomas B. Macaulay, *The History of England,* vol. 1. Longman, 1856, p.88.
28. Neal, *History of the Puritans,* vol. 1, pp.538ff.
29. Spurr, *English Puritanism,* p.91.
30. *Ibid,* pp.117ff.A
31. Antonia Fraser, *Cromwell our Chief of Men,* 1975, Panther, p.390.
32. Michael A. G. Haykin, *Kiffin, Knollys and Keach, Rediscovering our Baptist Heritage,* Carey Publications, 1996.
33. John Bunyan's *Complete Works* is published in three large handsome volumes by the Banner of Truth Trust, and by the same publisher the very popular *Body of Divinity* by Thomas Watson and Richard Baxter's *The Reformed Pastor*, the latter as a paperback.
34. Hylson-Smith, *Churches in England,* p.225; cf. Spurr, *English Puritanism,* p.118.
35. D. Martyn Lloyd-Jones, *From Puritanism to Nonconformity,* provides a stirring account of the Great Ejection and its implications (Evangelical Library Lecture for 1962).
36. David L Wykes, *To Revive the Memory of Some Excellent Men* (Dr Williams Library Lecture for 1997). This paper approaches to the most accurate count for the 1662 Ejection that we are ever likely to achieve. Dr Wykes outlines the history of biography on this subject with special reference to Edmund Calamy's work, Edmund Calamy being the grandson of the well-known Puritan of the same name.
37. Thomas Doolittle's sermon 'Eyeing Eternity' is found in volume 4 of the large six-volume set known as *The Morning Exercises, sermons preached by the Puritans at Cripplegate, London,* published by Richard Owen Roberts, Wheaton, Illinois, 1981. 'Eyeing Eternity', it has been suggested, may be the most awesome Puritan sermon ever preached! Thomas Doolittle's work on the ordinance of the Lord's Supper was published by *Soli Deo Gloria* in 1998.
38. Sinclair Ferguson, *John Owen on the Christian Life,* Banner of Truth, 1987, p.19.

39. D. Martyn Lloyd-Jones, *Puritan Perplexities,* Puritan Conference Paper, 1962.
40. J. I. Packer, *Among God's Giants, The Puritan vision of the Christian Life,* Kingsway 1991, pp.41ff.
41. Geoffrey F. Nuttall, *The Holy Spirit in Puritan Faith and Experience,* Chicago University Press, 1992.
42. Packer, *Among God's Giants,* p.45.

Part II — The lives of the Puritans

1. Haller, *The Rise of Puritanism*, p.55.
2. These titles by Robert Bolton have been reprinted by *Soli Deo Gloria.*
3. *The Rare Jewel* is kept in print by the Banner of Truth Trust.
4. These titles by Burroughs have been reprinted by *Soli Deo Gloria.*
5. Burroughs' treatise on Hosea was published by *Soli Deo Gloria* during the early 1990s but the entire edition sold out. *Irenicum* is published by *Soli Deo Gloria.*
6. Reprinted by the Banner of Truth Trust.
7. 1997 edition by the Banner of Truth Trust.
8. These titles are kept in print by the Banner of Truth Trust. *Soli Deo Gloria* has published writings by Thomas Watson: *The Sermons of Thomas Watson, The Art of Divine Contentment, Gleanings from Thomas Watson, Heaven Taken by Storm.* Unpublished Treatises by Watson are *Jerusalem's Glory*, a copy of which is at Dr Williams' Library in London, and *The Witnesses Anatomized*, the only known copy to exist being at Dulwich College in London.
9. These materials are published as popular paperbacks by the Banner of Truth Trust.
10. John Blanchard has produced a version of Baxter's *Call to the Unconverted* in modern English and called it *An Invitation to Live.* This useful paperback is published by Evangelical Press.
11. Bunyan's complete works have been published in three handsome large illustrated volumes by the Banner of Truth Trust
12. 1968 edition published by the Banner of Truth Trust.
13. Flavel's work on providence is published as a popular paperback by the Banner of Truth Trust.
14. First published in 1724 in two volumes; reissued in three volumes in 1848, reprinted in 1990 by *Soli Deo Gloria.* Included are two of his most famous expositions, *Delighting in God*, and *The Redeemer's Tears Shed over Lost Souls.* Somehow fifteen sermons on Ezekiel by Howe were missed out of the three-volume set. They were reprinted separately by the Religious Tract Society under the title *The Outpouring of the Holy Spirit* with a sub-title, *The Prosperous State of the Christian Interest Before the End of Time, by a Plentiful Effusion of the Holy Spirit*
15. The two volumes of the *Lives of Philip and Matthew Henry* (416 pages and 310 pages) were republished in one volume in 1974 by the Banner of Truth Trust.
16. Ernest W Bacon, *Spurgeon — Heir of the Puritans*, Eerdmans, 1968, p.7.
17. C. H. Spurgeon, *The Early Years*, Banner of Truth, 1962, p.11.
18. For a description of this renewal see Robert Oliver's Evangelical Library publication *Our Glorious Heritage, The Recovery of the Reformed Faith in the Twentieth Century,* and the article, 'The Theological Renewal 1950-2000', by Erroll Hulse, in *Reformation Today* 162.
19. D. Martyn Lloyd-Jones, *The Puritans*, Banner of Truth, 417 pp., 1987.
20. J. I. Packer, *Among God's Giants, Aspects of Puritan Christianity*, Kingsway, 442 pp., 1991.

Part III — Help from the Puritans

Chapter 1 — The Westminster Conference and Justification

1. Thomas Watson, *Body of Divinity*, Banner of Truth, 1970, p.226.
2. John Owen, *Works*, vol. 5, Banner of Truth, 1965.
3. Martin Luther, *What Luther Says: An Anthology*, vol. 2, pp.702ff., cited in *Foundations of the Christian Faith*, James Montgomery Boice, IVP, 1986.
4. Owen, *Works*, vol. 5, pp.321 ff.
5. E. P. Sanders' treatise *Paul and Palestinian Judaism*, 1977, has made a major impact on New Testament scholarship. Sanders' thesis was that Judaism of the first century was not a religion of works. I am entirely unimpressed by his thesis since it flies in the face of what the New Testament everywhere asserts and also because Sanders rests his case on very limited data.
6. Watson, *Body of Divinity*, p.227.
7. Owen, *Works*, vol. 5, pp.125ff.
8. William Bridge, *Works*, vol. 5, *Soli Deo Gloria,* p.378.
9. Thomas Goodwin, *Works*, Banner of Truth, vol. 8.
10. Alister McGrath, *Iustitia Dei*, Cambridge, is a major work (532 pages) describing the doctrine of justification and the place of that doctrine in the history of the church from Augustine to recent ecumenical debates.
11. Robert Traill (1642-1716) defended the doctrine of justification in six sermons on Galatians 2:21, *Works*, vol. 4, pp.157ff.
12. Owen, *Works*, vol. 5, pp.137ff.
13. Philip Eveson, *The Great Exchange — Justification by faith in the light of recent thought*, Day One Publications, 1996 (225 pp.). The author briefly reviews justification as it is presented in the new *Catechism of the Catholic Church,* Geoffrey Chapman, 1994 (690 pp.).
14. Owen, *Works*, vol. 5, pp.137ff.
15. A report on the Philippines by Noel Espinosa was emailed in April 1999 to Roger Fay of the *Evangelical Times.*
16. Owen, *Works,* vol. 5, pp.100.
17. *apokaluptetai,* ' is being revealed' — the verb is a frequentative present.

Chapter 2 — The Puritans and a stable doctrine of divine sovereignty and human responsibility

1. Spurgeon, an heir of the Puritans, fought the battle against both Arminianism and hyper-Calvinism. Iain Murray brilliantly sums up the issues involved in his book *Spurgeon v. Hyper-Calvinism — The Battle for Gospel Preaching*, Banner of Truth, 1995, 164pp.
2. J. I. Packer, *Evangelism and the Sovereignty of God*, was first published by IVP in 1961. It is currently available as a 128-page paperback.
3. *A Faith to Confess,* Carey Publications, 1997, p.31.
4. J. I. Packer and O. R. Johnston in the introduction to the new translation of Martin Luther's *The Bondage of the Will,* James Clark, London, 1957.
5. Kent Philpott, *Are You Really Born Again*? Evangelical Press, 1998, 144pp.
6. Erroll Hulse, *The Great Invitation*, Evangelical Press, 1986, 192 pp. The biblical warrant or otherwise for the appeal, or altar call, and the history of that practice are discussed.
7. William Greenhill, sermon in *The Morning Exercises at Cripplegate,* vol. 1, p.38.
8. John Blanchard, *Invitation to Live, a modernization of Richard's Baxter's* Call to the Unconverted *for today's reader*, Evangelical Press, 144 pp.

9. Robert Bolton, *Instructions for a Right Comforting of Afflicted Consciences*, 1640 edition, p.185.
10. John Flavel, *Works*, vol. 4, Banner of Truth. A 400-page paperback was published by Baker Book House in 1978 with the title *Christ Knocking at the Door of Sinners' Hearts.*
11. Two articles in the *Banner of Truth* magazine pointed the way for the recovery of the Reformed faith in England. In June 1958 (issue 11) the free offer of the gospel was clearly expounded. In February 1959 an exposition was republished by John Bonar with the title *Universal Gospel Invitations Consistent with Total Depravity and Particular Redemption*. In this way Puritanism was placed in the driving seat as far as gospel preaching is concerned.
12. Bob Sheehan expounds on this theme in 'Is there a love of God for all mankind?' *Reformation Today* 138, and 'God's love for the non-elect', *Reformation Today* 145. The subject is developed further in *Reformation Today* 135 in an article entitled 'John 3:16 and Hyper-Calvinism'.
13. John Howe, *Works*, *Soli Deo Gloria,* 1990, vol. 2, pp.316ff.

Chapter 3 — The recovery of the Lord's Day

1. The best contemporary treatment in a short compass today is Joseph A Pipa's *The Lord's Day*, Christian Focus, 1997, 252 pp. See also Packer, *Among God's Giants*, pp.309ff., and Erroll Hulse, 'Sanctifying the Lord's Day: Reformed and Puritan Attitudes', *Westminster Conference Papers* 1981.
2. These quotations are from John Blanchard's *Gathered Gold,* Evangelical Press, 1984.
3. Patrick Collinson, 'The Beginnings of English Sabbatarianism', 1964, an article which appeared in an American periodical *Studies in Church History*, vol. 1, pp.207-21.
4. Neal, *History of the Puritans*, vol. 1, p.560.
5. *Ibid.,* p.367.
6. Nicholas Bownde, early edition in British Museum, p.132.
7. George Swinnock, *Works*, vol. 1, Banner of Truth, 1992, p.222.
8. Thomas Watson, *The Ten Commandments*, Banner of Truth, p.97.

Chapter 4 — Marriage and the family

1. Thomas K Johnson, 'Responding to the Sexual Revolution', *Outlook* magazine, March 1998, USA.
2. Packer, *Among God's Giants*, p.342.
3. William Gouge, *Domestical Duties*, 1634, 600 pp.
4. Thomas Manton, *Works*, vol. 19.
5. D. Martyn Lloyd-Jones, *Marriage, Home and Work*, Banner of Truth, 1974.
6. Thomas Gataker, *A Wife Indeed*, Schnuker, pp.139-40.
7. Thomas Manton in a wedding sermon on Genesis 2:22, *Works*, vol. 2, Banner of Truth, pp.162ff.
8. Swinnock, *Works,* vol. 1, p.467.
9. Richard Sibbes cited in Leland Ryken's *Worldly Saints*, Zondervan, 1986, p.42.
10. Ryken, *Worldly Saints*, p.78.
11. *Ibid*, p.80.
12. *Ibid.,* p.81.
13. Richard Baxter, *The Poor Man's Family Book*, Baxter's *Practical Works*, vol. 4, pp.165-289.

Chapter 5 — A biblical basis for spiritual experience

1. Gaius Davies, 'The Toronto Blessing, a discussion', *Reformation Today* 144.
2. Flavel, *Works*, vol. 3, pp.57-8.
3. Jonathan Edwards, *The Religious Affections*, Banner of Truth, 1961, 382 pp.
4. *Ibid.,* p.23.
5. Thomas Manton, 'On rejoicing in God at all times and under all conditions, two sermons on 1 Thessalonians 5:16,' vol. 17, pp.469-89. Thomas Vincent, 'Concerning Christ's manifestations of himself to them that love him', an appendix *to The True Christian's Love to the Unseen Christ,* pp.100-127. William Bridge, *A Lifting up for the Downcast*, Banner of Truth, 287 pp. Joseph Symonds, *The Case and Cure of a Deserted Soul, Soli Deo Gloria*, 346 pp. Jeremiah Burroughs, *The Rare Jewel of Christian Contentment*, Banner of Truth, 228 pp. Thomas Brooks, 'The Mute Christian Under the Smarting Rod,' *Works*, vol. 1, pp.415-597.
6. John Owen, *Communion with God*, abridged to an easy-to-read 200-page paperback by R. J. K. Law, Banner of Truth, 1991.
7. Howe, *Works*, vol. 1, pp.474-664.
8. Thomas Brooks, *Works*, Banner of Truth, vol.2, pp.11ff.
9. Thomas Brooks, *Heaven on Earth*, Banner of Truth, p.139.

Chapter 6 — A robust doctrine of assurance

1. Thomas Brooks, *Heaven on Earth, A Treatise on Christian Assurance*, Banner of Truth, 319pp. The first modern reprint of this work, which was first published in 1654, appeared in 1961. At the time of writing the most recent reprint is dated 1996.
2. *Ibid.*, pp.14-15.
3. Joel Beeke, *Assurance of Faith, Calvin, English Puritanism, and the Dutch Second Reformation*, Peter Lang Publishers. 518 pp. Joel Beeke's treatise is very thorough but readable and edifying throughout. A shorter treatment by Beeke of the *Westminster Confession* chapter on assurance can be found in the *Westminster Conference Papers* for 1997 under the title 'Anthony Burgess on Assurance'.
4. The two leading 'non-lordship' authors are Charles C Ryrie, *So Great Salvation*, Victor Books, Wheaton, USA, 1989, and Zane C Hodges, *Absolutely Free! A Biblical Reply to Lordship Salvation*, Dallas: Recension Viva, 1989. The best-known book defending the view that a Christian must have Christ as both Saviour and Lord is John MacArthur's *The Gospel According to Jesus,* Zondervan, 1988. Highly recommended is *Lordship Salvation* by Robert Lescelius, Revival Literature, USA, 1992, 217pp. This book has the advantage of holding the previously mentioned titles in view and is a model of lucidity in the Puritan tradition. A fine study by Ernest Reisinger, *Lord and Christ*, was published by Presbyterian & Reformed in 1994 (178 pp.). The latter is commended especially for the section which explains the confusion wrought by Dispensationalism and for the chapter on assurance.

Chapter 7 — Hope for the future of the church

1. The Puritan hope was taken up and expounded by Jonathan Edwards in his book *The History of Redemption*. Edwards earned the title 'the Theologian of Revival'. Several modern expositions which develop 'the Puritan hope' are available today. See Iain Murray, *The Puritan Hope*, Banner of Truth, 328 pp.; Marcellus Kik, *An Eschatology of Victory*, Presbyterian & Reformed, 268 pp.; John Jefferson Davis, *The Victory of Christ's Kingdom,* Canon Press, 92 pp.; and Erroll Hulse, *Give Him No Rest*, Evangelical Press, 144 pp.

2. Edward Reynolds, *An Exposition of Psalm 110*, vol. 2, *Soli Deo Gloria*, 1993, p.25.
3. While the Puritans varied in their views on eschatology, most would be labelled postmillennial, believing, not that there is a specific period of 1,000 years, but rather that Christ would return only after the world has been evangelized. A minority were premillennial, the best-known of these being Thomas Goodwin, William Twisse, Jeremiah Burroughs and William Bridge. They taught that Christ will come personally to fulfil the grand promises that are made concerning the extension of his kingdom. Both these views do not spiritualize away the promises as mere poetry, but rather grapple with them.
4. Thomas Manton, *Works*, vol. 3, cf. *The Westminster Confession of Faith* ch. 25, para. 6 and *The 1689 London Baptist Confession*, ch. 26, para. 4.
5. Owen, *Works*, vol. 14, pp.241ff, 534ff.
6. John Howe's 'Prosperous State' is not included in his three-volume *Works* but is published as an appendix in Iain Murray's *The Puritan Hope*.
7. Elnathan Parr, *An Exposition of the Epistle to the Romans.* My copy is an edition published in 1651; Romans chapter 11 occupies pages 138-83.
8. Charles Hodge, Robert Haldane, Frederic Louis Godet, Prof. John Murray, Leon Morris and James Dunn are among commentators who stress the contextual argument developed by Paul in Romans 11. Godet refers to 'the two portions of mankind which Paul has been contrasting with each other throughout the whole chapter. St Paul teaches only one thing here: that at the close of the history of mankind on this earth there will be an economy of grace in which salvation will be extended to the totality of the nations living here below.'

Chapter 8 — The warrant of faith and the way to faith
1. Cotton Mather, *The Great Works of Christ in America*, vol. 1, Banner of Truth, 1979, p.335.
2. The subject of preparation is discussed helpfully by Robert Horn in 'Thomas Hooker — The Soul's Preparation for Christ', *Westminster Conference Papers* 1976, and by Iain Murray in a series of articles in the *Banner of Truth* magazine, issues 195, 196, 197, 199, 206.

Chapter 9 — The primacy of preaching
1. J. I. Packer, in his article 'Puritan Preaching' (*Reformation Today*, 68), outlines four axioms:

1. The primacy of the intellect;
2. The supreme importance (primacy) of preaching;
3. Belief in the life-giving power of biblical truths;
4. The sovereignty of the Holy Spirit.

With regard to the first, compared to our feelings-centred age, the Puritans were robust in their demands on the mind, but I do not think for one moment that they were self-consciously saying, 'I must direct this to the mind.' In his writings on the Puritans, Packer shows that hearers were addressed affectionately and intellectually (cf. *Among God's Giants*, p.79).

Geoff Thomas says, 'One of the great perils that face preachers of the reformed faith is the problem of a hyper-intellectualism, that is, the constant danger of lapsing into a purely cerebral form of

proclamation, which falls exclusively upon the intellect. Men become obsessed with doctrine and end up brain-oriented preachers. There is consequently a fearful impoverishment in their hearers emotionally, devotionally and practically. Such pastors are men of books and not men of people; they know doctrines, but they know nothing of the emotional side of religion. They set little store upon experience or upon constant fellowship and interaction with almighty God' (from the book *Preaching*, Evangelical Press, p.369).
2. Arthur Hildersam, *Lectures on Psalm 51*, folio, 1642, p.732.
3. Howe, *Works*, vol. 3, pp.389ff.

Chapter 11 — The reality of sin
1. John F MacArthur Jr, *The Vanishing Conscience*, Word Publishers, 1994, 280 pp.
2. Jeremiah Burroughs (1599-1646), *The Evil of Evils — The Exceeding Sinfulness of Sin*. His book first appeared in 1654 and was republished by *Soli Deo Gloria*, in 1992.
3. Ralph Venning was an outstanding preacher. His book *The Plague of Plagues* was republished by the Banner of Truth in 1993 with the title *The Sinfulness of Sin*.
4. Edward Reynolds, *The Sinfulness of Sin*, *Soli Deo Gloria,* 1992, pp.114ff.
5. This paragraph is cited from Ernest F. Kevan's outstanding book *The Grace of Law* published in 1976 by Baker Book House. A valuable service has been rendered by the publication of a new edition by *Soli Deo Gloria*.
6. Goodwin, *Works*, vol. 10.
7. David Clarkson (1621-1686), who followed John Owen in his last pastorate, wrote on original sin in an exposition of Psalm 51:5 (*Works,* vol. 1, pp.3-15). Also Thomas Watson (*Body of Divinity*, pp.139-46), John Flavel (*Works,* vol. 6, pp.172ff), John Owen (*Works,* vol. 2, p.64, and vol. 10, pp.68-82, in which he shows that Arminians deny the doctrine of original sin).

In the tradition of the Puritans see also the *Works of Thomas Boston*, vol. 1, pp.1-256 (The twelve volumes of Boston's *Works* were published by Richard Owen Roberts in 1980). Jonathan Edwards expounded the doctrine of original sin in depth (*Works*, vol. 1, Banner of Truth, 1974, pp.146-233).
8. *A Faith to Confess — The Baptist Confession of Faith of 1689 rewritten in modern English*, Carey Publications, 1975, pp.25-6.
9. Wayne Grudem, *Systematic Theology*, IVP, 1994, pp.494ff. Grudem gives sound reasons for using the term 'inherited sin' in lieu of 'original sin'. The phrase 'inherited sin' brings home more forcibly the sin that is ours as a result of Adam's fall.
10. Thomas Watson, *A Body of Divinity*, Banner of Truth. Watson's analysis of Adam's sin is highly commended (pp.142 ff.).
11. Stephen Charnock, *Works*, Parsons' edition, 1815, vol. 6, pp.289ff.
12. Thomas Manton, cited in Arthur W. Pink's, *Man's Total Depravity,* Moody Bible Institute of Chicago, 1969.
13. Herman Bavinck, *Gereformeerde Dogmatiek*, 111, p.29.
14. Owen, *Works*, vol. 6, p.5.
15. Manton, *Works*, vol. 1, p.266.
16. Obadiah Sedgwick, *The Anatomy of Secret Sins*, *Soli Deo Gloria,* 1995.
17. Venning, *The Sinfulness of Sin,* pp.106ff.
18. *Ibid.*, pp.84ff.
19. *Ibid.*, pp.71ff.
20. John Flavel, *Works*, vol. 3, p.133.

21. Swinnock, *Works*, vol. 5, p.456.
22. Richard Adams, *Puritan Sermons — Morning Exercises at Cripplegate*, Richard Owen Roberts, USA, 1981, vol. 5, pp.471ff.

Appendix I — Were the Puritans narrow-minded bigots?

1. Leland Ryken, *Worldly Saints — The Puritans as they Really Were,* Zondervan, 1986, 281pp.
2. In 1990 Baker Book House published an excellent book by Allen Carden called *Puritan Christianity in America — Religion and Life in Seventeenth Century Massachusetts.*

Appendix II — How do Baptists relate to the Puritans?

1. M. Haykin, *Kiffin, Knolly and Keach,* 1996, a *Reformation Today* title available from Evangelical Press.
2. Erroll Hulse, *Our Baptist Heritage,* Chapel Library, 1993.
3. Michael Watts, *The Dissenters — From the Reformation to the French Revolution,* Oxford, 1978, 542 pp.
4. James McGoldrick, *Baptist Successionism — A Crucial Question in Baptist History,* Atlanta, 1994.

Appendix III — Oxford and Cambridge universities

1. Alan B. Cobban, *The Medieval English Universities: Oxford and Cambridge,* Scolar Press, 1988.

Appendix IV — The Reformation in Scotland

1. Alexander Smellie, *Men of the Covenant,* Banner of Truth, 525 pp.

Select bibliography

I preface this brief bibliography by drawing attention again to the Evangelical Library, London, a wonderful source of Puritan books.

Attention is also drawn to *The Finder*, a combined author/ title index to three Reformed sources: *The Banner of Truth* magazine, 1955-1997, *Reformation Today* magazine, 1970-1997, and the Westminster /Puritan Conference 1956-1997. This index is compiled by Michael Keen and published by Tentmaker Publications of Stoke on Trent, Staffs. It is also available in electronic form on diskette. There are three pages of entries for the Puritans and Puritanism. *The Puritan Brotherhood* by John J. Murray, 1991, is especially recommended.

For contemporary scholarship on the Puritan period I have found Kenneth Hylson-Smith (Bursar and Fellow of St Cross College, Oxford), John Spurr (Senior Lecturer in History, University of Wales, Swansea) and Michael Watts (Reader in Modern History at the University of Nottingham), most helpful. *The Nature of the English Revolution*, essays by John Morrill, explains in fine detail what happened in Britain in the mid-seventeenth century. John Morrill is Reader in Early Modern History and a Fellow a Fellow of Selwyn College, Cambridge.

ASHLEY, MAURICE. *The English Civil War — A Concise History with 169 illustrations*, Thames and Hudson, 1974, 190 pp.

BARKER, WILLIAM. *Puritan Profiles — 54 Puritans,* Christian Focus, 1996, 320 pp.

BEEKE, JOEL R. *Assurance of Faith — Calvin, English Puritanism and the Dutch Second Reformation,* Peter Lang publishers, 1994, 518 pp.

BINDOFF, S. T. *Tudor England,* Penguin, 1985, 319 pp.

BROOK, BENJAMIN. *The Lives of the Puritans, Soli Deo Gloria.* Brook gives us 450 biographies in three volumes, 1,500 pp.

CARDEN, ALLEN. *Puritan Christianity in America, Religion and Life in Seventeenth Century Massachusetts,* Baker, 1990, 220 pp.

CARRUTHERS, S. W. *The Everyday Work of the Westminster Assembly,* edited by J. Ligon Duncan III, Reformed Academic Press, USA, 1994, 282 pp.

CARSON, JOHN I. and HALL, DAVID W. *To Glorify and Enjoy God,* Banner of Truth, 1994, 338 pp. Essays on the history and grand themes of the Westminster Assembly

CLIFFE, J. T. *The Puritan Gentry — The Great Puritan Families of Early Stuart England,* Routledge and Kegan Paul, 1984, 312 pp.

COLLINSON, PATRICK. *The Elizabethan Puritan Movement,* Jonathan Cape, 1967, 525 pp.

COLLINSON, PATRICK. *Godly People — Essays on English Protestantism and Puritanism,* Hambledon Press, 1983, 590 pp.

COWARD, BARRY. *Oliver Cromwell,* Longman, 1991, 201 pp. Clear and concise. Highly commended to those who wish to be introduced to Cromwell.

DAVIES, HORTON. *The Worship of the English Puritans, Soli Deo Gloria,* 1997 (first published 1948), 303 pp.

FERGUSON, SINCLAIR. *John Owen and the Christian Life,* Banner of Truth, 1987, 298 pp. Highly commended.

FRASER, ANTONIA. *Cromwell our Chief of Men,* Panther, 1975, 774 pp.

GREEN, J. R. *A Short History of the English People,* Macmillan, 1909, [1878], 872 pp.

GREGORY, J. *Puritanism in the Old World and in the New,* Fleming, 1896.

HALLER, WILLIAM. *Foxe's Book of Martyrs and the Elect Nation,* Jonathan Cape, 1963, 258 pp. A superb book which should be kept in print.

HALLER, WILLIAM. *The Rise of Puritanism,* published in 1938 and now difficult to find. This is an important work describing the Puritan brotherhood which, like the previous one, ought to be kept in print.

HAYKIN, MICHAEL A. G. *Kiffin, Knollys and Keach,* Reformation Today Trust (distributed by Evangelical Press), 1996, 125 pp.

HERON, JAMES. *A Short History of Puritanism,* T. and T. Clark, 1908, 236 pp.

HETHERINGTON, WILLIAM M. *History of the Westminster Assembly of Divines,* 1843, republished by Still Waters Revival Books, 1993, 408 pp.

HILL, CHRISTOPHER. *The Century of Revolution 1603-1714,* Cardinal, 1974.

HILL, CHRISTOPHER. *God's Englishman — Oliver Cromwell and the English Revolution,* Penguin, 1970, 318 pp.

HILL, CHRISTOPHER. *A Nation of Change and Novelty — Radical Politics, Religion and Literature in 17th Century England,* Routledge, 1990, 272 pp.

HINDSON, EDWARD. *Introduction to Puritan Theology,* consisting of twelve selections from Puritan writings and an introduction by J. I. Packer, Baker, 1976, 282 pp. (The choice for eschatology is from Jonathan Edwards, 'The portion of the wicked and the portion of the righteous'.)

HULSE, ERROLL. *Our Baptist Heritage — Essay on the 1689 Confession and its Development,* Chapel Library, 1993, 30 pp.

HYLSON-SMITH, KENNETH. *The Churches in England from Elizabeth I to Elizabeth II, volume 1, 1558-1688.* SCM, 1996, 348 pp. Very readable. A tremendous amount of research is reflected in the seventeen-page bibliography

KNAPPEN, M. M. *Tudor Puritanism,* Chicago Press, 1965, 554 pp.

LEWIS, PETER. *The Genius of Puritanism,* Carey Publications 1976, *Soli Deo Gloria,* 1996, 144 pp.

LLOYD-JONES, D. MARTYN. *From Puritanism to Nonconformity.* The annual lecture of the Evangelical Library for 1962, published by the Evangelical Press of Wales, 48 pp.

LLOYD-JONES, D. MARTYN. *The Puritans — Addresses delivered at the Puritan and Westminster Conferences 1959-1978,* Banner of Truth, 19 papers, 1987, 421 pp.

LUPTON, LEWIS. *History of the Geneva Bible,* 25 vols, The Olive Tree, 1966-1994, Wonderfully illustrated throughout by the author. Volumes vary in size from 120 to 250 pp. For this unique set consult the Evangelical Library, London.

MACAULAY, THOMAS B. *The History of England,* vol. 1, 11th edition, Longman, 1856, 684 pp.

MARTIN, ROBERT P. *A Guide to the Puritans.* A comprehensive listing of Puritan writings available today which reflects the revival of interest in Puritan literature, Banner of Truth, 1997, 530 pp.

MATHER, COTTON. *The Great Works of Christ in America,* Banner of Truth, 1979, 2 vols, each 620 pp.

MITCHELL, ALEXANDER F. *The Westminster Assembly — Its History and Standards.* The Baird Lecture for 1882, republished in 1992 by Still Waters Revival Books, 518 pp.

MOZLEY, J. F. *John Foxe and his Book,* 1940. Sadly the Evangelical Library, London, report that their copy of this important volume is missing.

NEAL, DANIEL. *The History of the Puritans,* 3 vols, totalling 1,975 pp., Klock and Klock, 1979. First published in 1731, it tells the political and ecclesiastical story from Henry VIII all the way through to the death of Charles II.

MORRILL, JOHN. *The Nature of the English Revolution — Essays,* Longman, 1993, 466 pp.

NUTTALL, GEOFFREY F. *The Holy Spirit in Puritan Faith and Experience,* Chicago University Press, 1992, 192 pp.

OLIVER, ROBERT W. *A Glorious Heritage — The Recovery of the Reformed Faith in 20th Century England.* The annual Evangelical Library lecture for 1997, 20 pp.

PACKER, J. I. *Among God's Giants — The Puritan vision of the Christian Life,* Kingsway, 1991, 446 pp. 19 papers, nearly all of which were first delivered at the Puritan Conference.

PAUL, ROBERT S. *The Assembly of the Lord, Politics and Religion in the Westminster Assembly,* T. and T. Clark, 1985, 609 pp. Describes the background and progress of the Assembly. Highly commended.

PORTER, H. C. *Reformation and Reaction in Tudor Cambridge,* CUP, 1958, 469 pp.

REID, JAMES. *Memoirs of the Westminster Divines,* Banner of Truth, two volumes in one, 756 pp. This is biographical with short accounts of those who attended the Assembly including the Scottish Commissioners.

RYKEN, LELAND. *The Puritans as they really were,* Zondervan, 1986, 281 pp.

SEAVER, PAUL S. *The Puritan Lectureships — The politics of religious dissent, 1560-1662,* Stanford University Press, 1970, 400 pp.

SPURR, JOHN. *English Puritanism 1603-1689,* Macmillan Press, 1998, 245 pp. An excellent work

STOWELL, W. H. *The Puritans in England,* Nelson, 1849, 334 pp.

TYACKE, NICHOLAS. *Anti-Calvinists — the Rise of English Arminianism c.1590-1640,* OUP, 1987, 305 pp.

TYACKE, NICHOLAS. *The Fortunes of English Puritanism, 1603-1640.* Lecture given for the Dr Williams Library, 1990, 23 pp.

TREVOR-ROPER, H. R. *Archbishop Laud 1573-1645,* Macmillan, 1940, 464 pp. Obtainable from Dr Williams Library, London.

TRUEMAN, CARL R. *Luther's Legacy — Salvation and the English Reformers, 1525-1556* (William Tyndale, John Frith, Robert Barnes, John Hooper and John Bradford), Oxford University Press, 1994, 307 pp.

WALLACE, DEWEY D. *The Spirituality of the later English Puritans,* Mercer University Press, 1987, 274 large size pp. This volume contains a valuable introduction on the subject of spirituality followed by extracts from the diaries and writings of about twenty Puritans.

WATKINS, OWEN C. T . *The Puritan Experience,* Routledge, 1972, 270 pp.

WATTS, MICHAEL. *The Dissenters — From the Reformation to the French Revolution,* Oxford University Press, 1978, 543 pp.

WEDGWOOD, C. V. *The King's Peace, 1637-1641,* Collins, 1969, 510 pp.

WEDGWOOD, C. V. *The King's War, 1641-1647,* Book Club Associates, London, 1974.

WHITE, B. R. *Hanserd Knollys and Radical Dissent in the 17th Century.* Dr Williams 1977 Library lecture, 24 pp.

WILSON, D. *The Pilgrim Fathers,* Nelson, 1849, 168 pp.

WYKES, DAVID L. *To Revive the Memory of some Excellent Men: Edmund Calamy and the early historians of Nonconformity,* Dr Williams 1997 Library lecture, 32 pp. Edmund Calamy, grandson of the Puritan of that name, worked extensively on gathering the details of the 1662 Ejection. This study by Dr Wykes describes the history of research and biographical writing on the 1662 Ejection.

VAN TIL, JOHN L. *Liberty of Conscience — The History of a Puritan Idea.* A well-researched book and enjoyable to read, Presbyterian & Reformed Publishing Co., 1992, 192 pp.

Index

A wide range of excellent books on spiritual subjects is available from Evangelical Press. Please write to us for your free catalogue or contact us by e-mail.

Evangelical Press
Faverdale North Industrial Estate, Darlington, Co. Durham, DL3 0PH, England

Evangelical Press USA
P. O. Box 84, Auburn, MA 01501, USA

e-mail: sales@evangelical-press.org

web: www.evangelical-press.org